*May this book honor the living memory of
Sr. Kieran Flynn, RSM (1915–1987),
a woman of Tradition, Mercy, and Vision
whose dream it was and is still
that every parish might become
a spiritual life center.*

PARISH ALIVE!

PARISH ALIVE!

≈

Making Every Parish a
Spiritual Life Center

FELICIA B. McKNIGHT

CROSSROAD • NEW YORK

1992

The Crossroad Publishing Company
370 Lexington Avenue, New York, NY 10017

Copyright © 1992 by Felicia B. McKnight

Printed in the United States of America
Typesetting output: TEXSource, Houston

Library of Congress Cataloging-in-Publication Data
McKnight, Felicia B.
    Parish alive : making every parish a spiritual life center /
Felicia B. McKnight.
        p.   cm.
    Include bibliographical references.
    ISBN 0-8245-1187-5
    1. Spirituality—Catholic Church. 2. Parishes. 3. Catholic
Church. Diocese of Providence (R.I.)   I. Title.
BX2350.65.M34   1992
250—dc20
                                              92-1209
                                                CIP

CONTENTS

PREFACE

Human transformation is the dancing partner of spirituality. The parish hall dance floor has expanded these days, pushing back the walls and ceiling; and the two who dance find the stars beneath their feet as well as above their heads. The music is a kind of rhapsody in cosmic colors; melody and harmonies intermingle a poignant reminiscence with a dominant theme of powerful expansion toward the very boundaries of nearly tomorrow. These two are clearly in love, and the music that binds them together will not be silenced, even should the small orchestra pack up its instruments and sheet music and go home. There's a timely chemistry at work in these two; one can't help but notice!

But have we in the church noticed, really noticed?

It is my contention that in the quarter century since Vatican II, the Catholic Church in the United States has plunged, with customary cultural energy, into the infinite sea of packaged renewal. Programs, designed to carry whole parishes headlong into the twentieth century (and I say that advisedly), abound from coast to coast. Institutional transformation is the avowed goal.... "Come to St. Someone's ... now, there's a real Vatican II parish!" often seems to mean that this parish as institution has moved from the monolithic to the something-in-it-for-everybody model of parish entertainment, from the divine right of kings to the model-town-meeting mode of institutional government (read parish council). Can it be that this first postconciliar generation has been merely a dress rehearsal for the twenty-first century?

Meanwhile, back in the world, the planet has discovered itself to be a singular and sacred living organism. The ground

9

has shifted under the feet of one common humanity that begins to see itself as the corporate consciousness of the planet
Earth. The electronic age has linked the far-flung stories and
memories and aspirations of the once diverse and dichotomized
citizenry of the worldwide hometown that is the Earth. In
the scientific community, a search is underway for a unifying spiritual principle that underlies the mega-mystery of the
ordered cosmic chaos. From the barrios of the Southern hemi-
sphere, where there is no longer any treasure to be measured
or weighed, except for the agony of poverty, the odor of sanctity arises like clouds of incense once did in the Eurocentric
church. In the space of one year, a seemingly impenetrable
socio-economic-political world order vaporizes and is blown
away like pebbles and dust, as the one voice of the oppressed
rises up for human freedom and dignity and becomes power
for transformation in Eastern Europe. The word becomes flesh:
"Father, may they all be one, as you and I are one, so the world
will know you sent me" (John 17:21).

The dance begins again, before our very eyes. The balance
of "things as they have always been" is upset. A new kind of
grace asserts itself, and the dancers' ordinary limitations yield
before strains of music freed now from long hidden recesses
in the human heart. And the very human heart of Jesus speaks
his prayer again across time — "Father, may they all be one...."
But *this* time, in *our* time, we can hear him pray, as we glimpse
the oneing that he sought, in the shifting paradigm of Earth's
imagination.

The initiation of transformation is no longer institutionally
based. Human transformation rests solidly with the individual human person. It is the large-scale collection and linking
of transformed individual human consciousnesses that form a
new corporate consciousness. In an older, and equally truthful
language, this personal transformation was called conversion of
life; it was accomplished through an in-depth spiritual journey
wherein the pilgrim met God, Self, and Others. The inward
journey is still the same, but the context of that journey has
transferred itself from private to common ground.

As I travel around the country to give retreats, workshops, wholistic parish missions, as I listen to people who come for spiritual direction, I see and hear a critical hunger in the men and women of the U.S. Catholic Church. It is a poverty in the midst of plenty for which people have few if any words. Still too subterranean for definition, it is expressed as a lived-out emptiness. In South Dakota, in Ohio, in Massachusetts; among poor and rich, young and old, religious and laity, the ordinary/ extraordinary People of God are starving for a living spirituality, for a taste of the reign of God, which St. Paul says, "...consists not merely of words but of power" (1 Thess. 1:5). They say that renewal programs were good, but didn't last. They say they don't know how to pray. They say they believe in small groups, if only some new people would come; they seem to be "spinning their wheels." They say of their parishes, "It's always the same people who do everything around here." They say, "My kids have a great time at CYO — if only they would go to Mass." They look at their church and ask, "Is that all there is?" They look at themselves and they ask, very secretly, "How can God love *me*?" They look and they look, but often there are only stale scraps that they find to feed their hunger.

No one seems able or willing to respond, "Yes, all of us are simply beggars in search of bread. One day, you are hungry, and I will show you where the bread is. On the next day, I will be hungry, and you will show me."

The spirituality of Incarnation; the concomitant understanding that human is holy, which creates mutual vulnerability; the spirituality of compassion equated with creativity; the spirituality of liberation from the oppression of false and limited self-image; the Trinitarian spirituality of dynamic relationship within the Godhead, mirrored by our own dynamic relationship with God, Self, and World; the many strands of spirituality in the woven beauty of our Tradition; spirituality that is a way of being and living—this food to feed the hungers of God's people is left uncultivated, unflowered, unavailable. And we go on, those on both sides of the conservative/liberal split in the U.S. Catholic Church, trying to renew and reform the structures on the parish and diocesan levels. Suffering from malnutrition as we are, we can't seem to get very much done.

The way lies beyond the ideological split. The answer is not spoken, but is experienced in the unfolding mystery of the dance. Human transformation awaits her dancing partner in every place where the parish yearns, even unconsciously, to perceive itself as the local face of Christ.

Are you a parish member, sitting in the pew, waiting, more or less alone, for Good News? Are you a religious or a lay professional church minister, directing a parish educational program for baptized unbelievers of the teenaged sort, finding that your annual conscription of volunteer catechists is registering a flat line on your monitor? Are you a faithful Altar and Rosary Society member who is beginning to wonder what making wreaths has to do with either the altar or the rosary? Are you a permanent deacon whose permanence is much ado about ceremonials and in-house status and little to do with ministry? Or are you a pastor whose high-wire budget-balancing act takes all the energy and skill you can muster away from your packed calendar of public appearances at the twenty-seven meetings per week of your various parish organizations? Have any of you pondered in the recent silence of your hearts, "Is that all there is...?" This book trusts your ponderings and your pain, and begins with your secret inner question about the meaning of your membership and leadership in the local church.

This book attempts, through the medium of a local story, with possibilities far beyond itself, to present the process of the dance that frees you to become more passionately alive as person and as parish. PARISH ALIVE! is not a linear renewal program with a clear time frame, precise goals, or uniform materials. Neither is it designed as a defined educational progression, wherein the parishioners of St. Someone's travel all together from Point A to Point Z. PARISH ALIVE! is a simultaneously multilayered, nonsymmetrical invitation to persons across the spectrum of parish life to grow in spirituality as individuals who travel from where they are as far as they want to go toward the embrace of transformation. PARISH ALIVE! is an invitation to expand the image of the parochial paradigm to a local-global locus of the church who is a person, the risen Christ, present in the transformed community.

PARISH ALIVE! is an invitation to the dance.

ACKNOWLEDGMENTS

I want to thank the following people for the various ways they were Christ's presence to me as I wrote this book:

- My colleagues at the Graduate Theological Foundation, Donaldson, Indiana, and particularly the foundation's president, Dr. John H. Morgan, and vice president, Rev. Robley Edward Whitson.

- My colleagues at Our Lady of Peace Spiritual Life Center, Narragansett, Rhode Island, particularly Fr. Robert Caul.

- Fr. John Allard, vicar for Spirituality and Evangelization, diocese of Providence.

- Michael Leach, publisher of Crossroad.

- Sally Donnelly, my patient, faithful friend and wizard at the keyboard.

- My four daughters, Mariclare, Sarah, Amanda, and Felicity, and my mother, Felicia Boxmann.

FELICIA B. MCKNIGHT

· 1 ·

WHERE DO YOU LIVE?

I LIVE BY THE OCEAN. Early this morning, as I walked along the sea-wall, I caught the unexpected glory of a rose and silver-gold sunrise edging from behind a rainy November Atlantic dawn. The tide was low and soft and shimmery, and every morning thing was as it should be. Sea birds hovered low in search of breakfast; clouds parted and the waves rolled in across the rocks in measured patterns of deep-souled sound and motion. All the elements of a simple seaside morning proclaimed God's glory: "See! We are who we are, all of what we are, nothing more and nothing less!" Waves, birds, sky, and earth — all agreed to be "perfect," that is, perfectly full of their own being, even as their Creator is perfectly full of who God is.

Just a mile down the road is the diocesan retreat house where I work. People from our diocese, as well as from other sections of our country (more than six thousand annually) come there, to the Spiritual Life Center, seeking an experience of God, of community, and of their own deeper selves. Most of those who come — laity, religious, and ordained — are "church people," ordinary/extra-ordinary people of God, looking for the "more," for the fullness of life that Jesus maintained he had come to bring. Often they find new definitions for old terms, fresh images of God, Self, and Others that better contain the deeper stirrings of their inner truth. Many have been taught in school and in religious formation that they are on a quest for perfection — "Be perfect, even as your Father in heaven is perfect" (Matt. 5:48) — but they have begun to suspect that these

17

words of Jesus are impossible to actualize...or perhaps have been distorted by time and place, confused with our cultural "myth of perfectability."

And so they come, disappointed by an imperfect church, an imperfect parish or diocese, an imperfect religious congregation, imperfect family, imperfect self. They come for spiritual direction, for retreats, for classes in Christian spirituality; they come to discover a more "perfect" way. But instead of prepackaged answers, they find deeper questions. Instead of sureties, they find creative possibilities of living with ambiguities. Instead of clearcut road maps to "perfection," they find alternate approaches to mystery. Instead of new laws or systems to live by, they find an invitation to a fully lived life.

The theology of spirituality, which visitors to the center encounter, is incarnational. It rests firmly in the words about the Word of God, Jesus Christ, arising from the Gospels. Spirituality is often falsely imagined to be an "it,"...a compartmentalized add-on to church life, an abstruse study of prayer methods, an elite mode of knowing reserved for the few. In reality, Christian spirituality is a Person-Encountered in the extension of the Incarnation that is daily human life, in this place, in this time. The Person of Christ has ascended out into the midst of his people; the kingdom resides, resounds, reflects, rejoices within us and among us, in our very midst — but hiddenly, so hiddenly. The best kept secret of our Tradition is that our baptism empowers each one of us to go deeper, cast our nets wider, to go beyond our organizational status quo of church belonging and become individually and corporately the living Christ.

In the Vatican II document *Lumen Gentium*, the church defines itself primarily as the Mystery of Person (chapter 1); the church is the Person of Christ who is Sacrament (sign and reality) of the Father. The Good News of our baptism is Emmanuel, God Is with Us, as close to us as our own personal humanity, as near to us as the touch of another's hand, as present as the divine Holy Spirit who lives within each of us.

Ordinarily, such startling news might well be expected to cause at least a liberating ripple in the ho-hum flow of ecclesial daily life. Can it be that the news has not been broadcast widely on the local level? So it appears, as more and more people throughout the Catholic Church in the United States seek out retreat programs, centers of spirituality, houses of prayer, places often far from their homes where they hope doors to the treasures of spirituality might be opened for them.

What of the others? What of those for whom the Retreat House on the Hill or the Center by the Sea are too distant, too costly, too unfamiliar? The wealth of spirituality is their inheritance too! Is it not conceivable then, that the most appropriate "center" for spirituality should be the place where the people are? And that place is the local parish. But with the business at hand, how can every parish possibly become a spiritual life center?

This felt need for spirituality, imprisoned in the human heart of the institutional church, seems most often to be a complex puzzle, insoluble and therefore largely untouched. In our diocese, the problem was perceived as a jigsaw puzzle with ragged or flaccid edges. Nine-tenths of the puzzle board was filled with a varied assortment of predictable pieces, the 159 parishes in the state. These parish pieces had been overlaid with many coats of color, the valiant efforts of various renewal programs, commonplace throughout our country for the last two and a half decades. Some renewal efforts, through these hundred seasons since the close of the Vatican Council, were too specialized, some too localized, some too homogenized — and all of them were aimed at renewing the institution. Color upon color was applied to our puzzle pieces, but no one shade pleased everyone, none just right, some fading fast. Some parish pieces were never painted with the new colors at all, as attested to by one parishioner's representative remark in the mid-1980s. At a public meeting for parents of Confirmation students, which stressed the youngsters' need to become acquainted with the "preferential option for the poor," this parent offered a heated response to the Director of Religious Education's presentation: "Stop that kind of talk in this church! Don't you know that Vatican II hasn't come to this town yet?" This unfortunately anachronistic retort, echoed in many other localities, was voiced and applauded in a parish that had just completed its second year of a packaged renewal program.

Another glance at the puzzle revealed a round, shiny puzzle piece, perceived as somewhat apart, irrelevant and other, when viewed as a possible match from the perspective of the parish pieces. Lying due south on the puzzle board, approximately forty-five minutes' driving time from the diocesan office building, is the diocesan retreat center. During these years of the 1970s and 1980s, a time of diminishing church attendance, clerical vocations, and budgets, the center had been flourishing. The Spiritual Life Center, down by the sea, had, in fact, grown from modest attempts at retreat work in the summer of 1978, when the bishop asked the center's two team members to move from the city to the ocean-front location, to a going concern of thirteen thousand person-days per year by 1989. Men and women from a tristate area were going there to a three-year Spirituality of Christian Leadership program; hundreds were coming for monthly spiritual direction appointments; there was a fifty-two-room retreat house, full nearly every weekend between September and Memorial Day — and full again through the consecutive eight-day directed retreats that run throughout the summer months; the four-unit hermitage had to be booked months in advance by prospective private retreatants, with stays ranging from a weekend to thirty-day retreats; professional interns trained there for a ministry of spirituality and returned home after their year of study and supervision to found satellite spirituality centers in places as far from New England as Belize and New Zealand; a wholistic center for prayer and the arts was envisioned and then supported by friends of the center to be established in an antique barn on the property. All that, and more, that had happened in those fifteen years was the fruit of the dreams of the center's visionary foundress, Sr. Kieran Flynn, RSM (d. August 30, 1987), who believed with the Council Fathers that "all are called to holiness" (*Lumen Gentium*, chap. 5) and made it her life's work to enflesh those dreams. Beginning with a small building in the city (1974–78) and then called by the bishop to the existing but then defunct diocesan retreat center, she and her intercongregational term of professional spiritual directors maintained their central dream of empowerment for the laity, through a wholistic, incarnational spirituality.

Fundamental to the dream was the notion that "every parish should become a spiritual life center," and to that end many attempts were made to create a "Center on Wheels" that would export programs to the local level. But the cloudy perception in the diocese was that the center existed for the few, and there was little collaboration from the parishes in a formal sense.

Finally, at the end of the 1980s, diocesan officials took a long hard look at the center and at the diocesan puzzle as a whole. Find a way, they instructed the center's director and team, to serve *this* diocese effectively! The puzzled perspective changed with that simple phrase, from the official benign toleration of the center's successful mission of spirituality to a mandate for interdependence between the local institutional church and the existing local resource for spiritual growth.

$$\approx$$

Reality remained the same. Perspective changed. The second-order change inherent in a shift of perspective carries with it the power of the creative breath of the Spirit. Such a shift has nothing to do with novelty and everything to do with having eyes to see and ears to hear and with calling things by their right names.

This seeing, hearing, and naming are prophetic senses, alive with the power to effect change. Moving beyond the stoic and steely maintenance of the status quo to disclose possible futures for a church life lived rather than merely tolerated is a process of developing these three senses.

Look at your own local church situation. Listen to its people. Name the reality you discover. How does that reality match

or mismatch the pattern of the Gospel Christ, the pattern of
promise for a life that is truly life, right here and now, in
the midst of the mess? What resources can you discover in
your own area, already in place, perhaps completely ignored or
at least underutilized, that might introduce the breath/breadth
of human life and longing to an ecclesial organization grown
rigid and artificial? Are you certain you have asked the right
questions? Have you remembered that Christianity has more
to do with *persons* becoming all they can be than with the
existence and pattern-preservation of a group or structure? I
wonder if it is probable that when our perspective shifts from
"parish renewal" to personal transformation through spirituality our parishes (*which after all are relevant only as arbitrary
places where people are gathered*) will come alive in proportion
to the human growth and evolution of sacred consciousness in
the lives of individual men and women?

With these questions as a basis, PARISH ALIVE! came into
being as a collaborative process between the Spiritual Life Center and our diocese. It is important to notice that the process
is based on "questions" rather than on answers, assumptions,
or beliefs. In the realm of spirituality, questions lead to deeper
questions, penetrating mystery, yet never imposing systems or
parameters of any kind on the limitless.

It was a simple matter to frame the process, once the "yes"
of collaboration was audible. After all, years of experience in
spirituality and spiritual direction at the center, and elsewhere,
had indicated to its team that spiritual hunger and homeless-
ness of the human heart are no respecters of ecclesial roles.
Priests, housewives, religious sisters, lawyers, college students,
in a long line of "here comes everybody," hunger and thirst
for the "more" that is within. So the first premise of the
PARISH ALIVE! process had to be the possibility of dynamic spiritual growth for individuals across the spectrum of parish folks,
from the pastor to last Easter season's initiate. The image of
the parish population transmutes from a pyramid of ascending
knowledge, holiness, and power to a circle of seekers and story-
tellers, called together by the words spoken early or late to each

one: "I baptize you in the name of the Father and of the Son and of the Holy Spirit."

The PARISH ALIVE! process begins therefore with each person exactly where he or she really is, seeking a fresh discovery of how God beholds her or him in this present moment. The divine beholding that is a knowing and a loving of real persons by a really personal God is obviously far from uniform; point zero of the process must then be a constellation of as many and as varied starting points as there are individuals in the parish. It is at this starting point that PARISH ALIVE! is at radical variance with conventional renewal programs, which all begin with step one and participants proceed together as a group to the predetermined goal. Conventional programs assess their own success by the *numbers* that stay with the program from start to finish. PARISH ALIVE!'s self-critique is concerned instead with *quality of life and freedom* as measured against St. Paul's standard, "The reign of God does not consist in words but in power," power to live and experience the divine presence in human activity, for all, be they among the clergy, the laity, or the unchurched. When numbers don't count, the emphasis is on reverence for the person, regardless of his or her parish role, as if he or she were the only one.

If the ministry of spirituality is to bloom one day from within each parish, individuals must first be enabled to experience a receptivity toward gifts that they might later share with others. There needs to be an atmosphere of inclusivity within the process that welcomes those in all stages of the spiritual journey and offers holy hospitality to every level of faith. How often have we heard, or perhaps spoken, generous phrases like these, while imagining a picture of those with "more" bending down in welcome and gift-giving to those with "less"? The inclusive process of which I speak does not believe that any of us possesses a claim to the authority of dividing the "haves" and "have-nots" in the realm of the interior journey. Rather, the point of departure for all of us is the simple truth that each one, by our participation in humanity, is a needy creature. Each one is wooed and led to the lonely, freeing moment

when we can look into the darkness at the mystery of the un-
seen Holy One and whisper, "You are God, and I am not!"
When we accede to that reality, we can openly and joyfully
share the blessings of poverty of spirit and mutual vulnerability.
So blessed, we recognize that we all share a single status, that
of the poor pilgrim, beloved for no good reason except God's
own reason. "You are my beloved son and daughter. Upon you
my favor rests" (see Mark 1:11).

Practically speaking, what this means for PARISH ALIVE! is
that pastors, assistant pastors, deacons, religious men and
women, DREs, parish council members, et al., as well as Joe Q.
Catholic in the pew, are all called to *deeper* holiness and
wholeness. The process is designed with that universal call
in the forefront. Six initial umbrella offerings appear in the
simple sunshine yellow brochure announcing the first year of
PARISH ALIVE!: *Come and See,* an outreach from the Spiritual Life Center to the pastors of parishes across the diocese;
Spirituality for the Edge of an Age, Sunday evenings in the
parishes for the general parish population; *Come Aside and
Rest Awhile,* Sunday afternoons of prayer and reflection at
the center for those parishioners who are conscious of a need
for deeper prayer experience, both personal and communal;
One in Mind and Heart, days of reflection and/or consultation for the professional parish staff, either at the center or
in the parish, to provide the staff with unifying, shared prayer
experience and to train them in facilitation for developing spirituality resources within the parish they serve; *A Season of
Refreshment,* seasonal weekend retreats at the center for groups
from various parishes, particularly meant to appeal to inten-
tional clusters of lay parish leaders who are seeking to grow
in mutuality of prayer and community, as well as to experience their place in the wider church; *Greater Things Than
I Shall You Do,* specifically for leaders of small groups or
basic communities within parishes. Although the latter two
offerings speak specifically to lay "leaders," either current or
potential, the central thrust of the entire process is preparation to understand and live the priesthood of the baptized.

This call echoes and reechoes through every facet of the PARISH ALIVE! process.

The task of the following chapters is to unfold the story of the initial year of PARISH ALIVE! in one diocese, by detailing the lived reality of each of the six areas named above. As you read our story, I propose that *you* participate in the process by imagining what PARISH ALIVE! might look like where you live.

· 2 ·

COME AND SEE

IN THE GOSPELS, especially St. Luke, the simple source point of Jesus' community and ministry of reconciliation is table fellowship. So little and so much, the expected and the startling take place around the table. All things worthy of human celebration, large and small, wind their ways to the feasting table. Once you have eaten with another, there is a bond between you both, a leveling point from which you cannot retreat to anonymity.

Who came to Jesus' lectures and courses and programs is a nonquestion. If we look at Luke's Gospel, the cogent question is instead, "With whom did Jesus eat?" The Pharisees and scribes of Luke 15 grumble forth an answer with their disdainful judgment. "This man, they said, welcomes sinners and eats with them." In Luke 19, Jesus refuses to talk Zaccheus's ear off about necessary changes. Rather, he insists that *he must* come to Zaccheus's house that day for lunch. What must have happened at *that* table to change the shrinking little traitor, lately of the sycamore tree, into the generous follower of the rabbi from Nazareth? What inner cord was struck by the reverence of fellowship that could never be touched by homily or condemnation?

It seems that Jesus made many of his best points at table, when both sinners and Pharisees could relax in the fullness, fragrance, and flavors of a good meal. The greater part of Luke's fourteenth chapter takes place during a Sabbath meal, at the home of one of the leading Pharisees who evidently sought Jesus as an "in" dinner guest that season. The stories Jesus told around that table had much to do with invitations to dine, with places of honor at table, and with attitudes toward the banquet. "Shall I send this invitation?" "Will I accept that invitation?" "Will I be noticed if I attend?" "What excuse will seem plausible, this time, for yet another irritating invitation?"

Yes, the basic human dodges, confusions, and ambivalence surrounding presence at the table have not altered in all these centuries. The most interesting attitude in Luke's tale of the invited guests who made excuses (14:15–24) was that of the host. He didn't take kindly, at all, to the indifference (which is, more so than hatred, the very opposite of love) of his friends, but neither did he stew for a moment in his rage, much less cancel the party. Take to the streets, he told his servant, and compel them to come in! Yes, that's right, whomever you might find! This banquet will go on as scheduled!

It is at that last Passover table, of course, that the simple, earthy bread mingles its nourishment with the Bread of Heaven. Which of Jesus' guests at that supper really knew what had happened? Much later, seemingly worlds of time and space away, around a table for three at the Emmaus village inn, that which was so obscure at Thursday's meal, so utterly defeated by Friday's loss, became light and victory without end. "Yes, we recognized him in the breaking of the bread" (Luke 24:35).

There's something key about table fellowship, some sacred secret about the willingness to share a meal. And so the first item in the PARISH ALIVE! brochure was not the date, time, or cost of the first talk or retreat. It was an invitation to dinner. "Come and See...Pastors are invited to join the Center team for a festive dinner and introduction to PARISH ALIVE!...Thursday, September 13th at 5:30 P.M."

Some people said, "You're lucky if you get *one!* Who's going to drive thirty minutes for dinner?" (Please remember, Rhode Island is diminutive; drivable distances are measured in fifteen-minute increments in a state where one and one-half hours, at the speed limit, will take you from northern to southern tip, and it's longer than it is wide.) Other people asked, "Don't you know that pastors disregard anything that isn't an absolute obligation? They're just too busy with parish business." Still others remarked, "They'll be suspicious that you want something, that is, if they ever read the little yellow brochure at all — what with their piles of official letters, pleas, requests, complaints, and genuine junk mail."

But there's nothing like a personal invitation! I sent our invitation directly to forty pastors, representatives of all the deaneries in our diocese. The yellow brochures were enclosed. Some responded that they would be out of the country, or at least the state, on the date of the dinner. Some claimed previous engagements in the line of duty. One said he wasn't interested. Others never responded at all.

I'd like to be able to claim that this initial response was not stressful, but the center chef was already dabbling with exciting new recipes for the occasion. Besides that, I'd just been to a two-day forum to which every priest in the diocese had been personally invited by the bishop, and I'd seen six in attendance. "September's a bad time of year," people said. "Every parish is just beginning all its new programs...lots of meetings and all that."

I took some small comfort from two factors: (1) Luke's Gospel gave me the last-minute alternative of walking into town and searching out the hungry in the hedges, who might, however, be difficult to find in this unseasonably summery September with everyone in these parts still basking at the beach. (2) The wonderfully supportive vicar for evangelization, within whose mission the center falls, had been so willing to honor my request to send personal letters to each of the forty recipients of our invitation. He had urged them fraternally to join him at the center to "Come and See." It was great that his letter had predated the invitations, to lay the groundwork. Did it matter that his letter also predated the replies noted above? I had also enjoyed a very positive meeting of minds with the diocesan coordinator of parish renewal who is working on a project with several parishes that are seeking to restructure into small groups or basic communities. She was excited about PAR-ISH ALIVE!, promised to be present at the dinner, and was eager to support it in conversation with those pastors with whom she currently works. Encouraged as I was by this early collaboration from "downtown," still the specter haunted me of all us organizer-collaborator types graciously entertaining ourselves at the September 13th dinner party.

In the previous year, as the diocesan evaluation of the center unfolded, there had been much talk from the Diocesan Task Force that it was not only parishioners who were largely unaware of the center's wholistic spirituality as a valuable resource at their disposal. This unawareness, they noted, persisted despite the more than three thousand brochures, containing descriptions of all center offerings, that are mailed to Rhode Island residents and parishes annually. No, they insisted, not just the parishioners, but pastors as well were either unfamiliar with or hostile toward this work of spirituality. A poll of diocesan priests was suggested and taken to discover whether this contention was grounded in solid reality or in rumor or mere conjecture. Ninety-five percent of the replies were positive concerning the center's work. For most, their affirming replies had to do with positive prayer and learning experiences that parishioners reported having enjoyed at the center. Others had attended one or more of the four annual diocesan priests' retreats that have the center as their site, but that utilize their own outside directors and formats, rather than the Spiritual Life Center's team and programs. The small percentage who responded negatively had no personal firsthand knowledge of the center at all.

This information, gathered during the year before PARISH ALIVE! was imagined or designed, surfaced the central reality that the pastors of the diocese had never received personal, diocesan encouragement to "own" the center as a spirituality resource for themselves or their people. It seemed that pastors, as well as parishioners, tended to hear the word "spirituality" as irrelevant, or perhaps even a little dangerous, to the flow of "normal" church life.

The "Come and See" dinner was conceived of as a door for the clergy that might open out onto the center and the work of spirituality in itself, as the deeply human, "user-friendly" reality it is. Spirituality and its epicenter, ongoing conversion, acquired a suspect reputation only in the modern era of the Western Christian Tradition, i.e., the sixteenth century. The simple realism and necessity of the Christian spiritual journey originates with Jesus' forthright invitation to "Come, follow *me*" and his self-identification in John, "I am the way, the truth and the life." Christian spirituality, in its origins then, is simply the meeting of a Person and the personally lived-out story of the ongoing way home with him, home to the truth of one's own inner being as loved creature, and the concomitant freedom to live the fullness of life that this Person, Jesus, has promised (John 10:10). Spirituality has everything to do with my life as it really is and nothing to do with a disembodied piety or "spiritualism."

The false dualism of body as base and spirit as exalted that infiltrated Western religious belief was not operative in Jesus nor in his Semitic roots, nor in the Apostolic Age, nor in the writings of Church Fathers until Augustine. Augustine's Neoplatonism, as well as his entanglement with the Manichaean lightness-darkness religious philosophy, introduced a major contradiction between the "spiritual" and all that was earthy and human. Confusion deepened too between Christian spirituality and the dominant culture, the Hellenic-rooted Roman Empire, which embraced, legalized, and subsumed Christianity from the fourth century on. Shadow-like, these external influences, among others such as vestiges of pre-Christian, European tribal religions, clung to the Christian spiritual reality, permeating it ever more deeply as centuries spiraled into the millennium. The powerful, living traditions of contemplation as the ordinary goal of prayer, spiritual journey accompanied by a spiritual director or soul's companion, mysticism, creation as revelation, the feminine as integral to God's nature, all became esoteric or dangerous memories. Abuses, persecution of the prophets of every century and locale, superstition, ignorance, societal shifting and chaos also coagulated in the shadow side of the evolving church. Finally, in the rational, modern Western Europe that developed rapidly after 1500, all that bordered on the mystical, the feminine, or the contemplative was surgically removed from the body of everyday Christian orthodoxy.

With deft efficiency, the Reformation and the Counter-Reformation alike successfully banished from the popular Christian imagination the notions that spring from the mystery of the Incarnation: human is holy, creation is sacred, art and creativity are expressions of the divine-human symbiosis, each fleshy human being is a beloved daughter or son in whom God is well pleased. "And the Word of God became *flesh* and pitched his tabernacle tent among us...": pious formula or earthy Truth? When empirical truth began to be spelled with the only capital "T," as the Age of Reason dawned, there developed a pervasive fear of the prerational or nonrational in connection with approved European religious practices. A cry of fanaticism arose against those whose prayer or spiritual style took the form of anything deeper than "devotional."

All that was birthed in Europe in the clear light of reason, empiricism, and acceptability became a transatlantic export to the New World. Jansenists and others feared the human body and the passions of the human spirit, while they extolled the detached and ethereal human soul; they railed against mystery and its "mumbo-jumbo," but popularized religious sentimentality. American Catholic practice from Lord Calvert's Baltimore through the mid-twentieth century was as subverted by the dominant culture of practicality, profit, power politics, and plain talk, as was the so-called Protestant ethic.

Religion is always and everywhere informed by the culture. Spirituality, on the other hand, seeks to draw the very limits of existence into the center of human life; spirituality is always and everywhere counter-cultural. Religion supports the status quo; spirituality challenges persons to move beyond it. Religion is safe; spirituality is dangerous, as dangerous as the Gospel it seeks to live. Freedom is the medium and the goal of spirituality. People freed to reimage God, Self, and the World in new ways are rather difficult to control and often cease to "fit" within the dominant system and its worldview. It is no wonder, then, that despite the attitudes and teachings of Vatican II, the structural church as a human organization has been slow to implement the council's passionate cry for recognition of the universal call to holiness. New methods, new systems, new language have all been approved for teaching, for community restructuring, for worship; but newness of life as the birthright of all the baptized, on every level, has not attracted the wholehearted attention of, nor implementation by, the in-house church structure.

So it was not merely the history of this particular Spiritual Life Center nor its relationship with this particular diocese that was affecting our sluggish receipt of acceptance to a September dinner party! Rejection doesn't seem quite so personal and pointed when you realize you are simply caught in the flow of a centuries-old ecclesial story of Status Quo versus the God of Surprise. A wise old monk once told me, "Do not be fooled by appearances; that is, what appears to be really real, is, for the most part, unreal, and what seems unreal to most folks is the really real." That wisdom, which, by the way, the same old monk defined as "sanctified common sense," is not as inscrutable as it seems on first glance. One thing the maxim does for me is to free me from the numbers game, which is an unholy invention of our consumer society — the "more is better" yardstick. Well mentored by my monk, I tend to look at "who," rather than "how many?"

When our ten dinner guests arrived, I saw, beside them, the thousands of people in their ten parishes. Each pastor who chose table fellowship that evening was there with us because, as a person, the deepest desire of his heart was his own living relationship with Jesus Christ and his hunger and thirst to share that with his people. Was it possible that these pastors were the "ten good men" of Genesis 18 for whom God agrees to spare the city? Even by the measure of contemporary statis-

tics, 25 percent of the invited guests had arrived, which beats
both the reported figure on dinner guests in Luke 14 and the
recent diocesan ratio. There are many more ways of "seeing"
than first meet the eye.

What I saw and heard that evening was sincere delight on
the part of the dinner guests as they quickly came to understand that there were no strings attached to the feast set before
them. Eight of us on the team, along with the vicar and the
parish renewal coordinator, made a one-to-one ratio with the
ten pastors. What a splendid opportunity to let each man know
that all this was just for him. Isn't that the way God deals
with each of us, one at a time, with complete attention? Can
you feel the ambiance created when there is a glad emphasis on
person rather than number? It is reflective of the atmosphere of
spirituality as distinct from the mores of the dominant religious
culture.

As hors d'oeuvres and dinner mellowed down toward dessert, the lively conversations about facts, foibles, and fancies
of local Catholic parish life yielded to a more plaintive note.
Pastors-as-persons, around the dining room, began to speak of
their frustrated desires for a richer spiritual dimension in the
life of their parishes. So many duties, such a schedule of sacramental as well as administrative tasks make "the more" of
spiritual formation difficult or impossible. It was not for want
of wanting that any of these fine men were deterred from the
ministerial role closest to their hearts and imaginations. Little by little, stories of occupational stress and the constraints
of time and calendar were told at each table. By the time that
coffee was poured, questions began to surface like, "So what do
you people have in mind?...I like the looks of what I saw in
your yellow brochure; can you tell me more of what it might
look like for my parish in the inner city?...Do you think
my people are really ready for this? They're a pretty conservative group. Where do you start with the people in my parish?
They're at all sorts of different levels, you know...."

The place to begin, I said as I stood up to introduce the
pastors to the workings of PARISH ALIVE!, is most definitely not

at the beginning. The place to begin is right in the middle of
things as they are. "Things as they are" include all the variables
and contradictions of life as it is, confusing, frightening, empty,
over-full, passionate, boring, needy, self-satisfied, and on and
on. All the polarities and questions without answers of real life
as it is lived in everybody's parish, in everybody's house, stand
in marked contrast to life "as it should be," which dictates beginning at the beginning with some arbitrary point of departure
for "renewing the parish." Beginning in the middle suggests the
thick of things in which we all find ourselves: interior, spiritual
things, relational things, financial and health things, communal
things, civic things, global things, cosmic things. Spirituality
has to do with the thick of all these things. When what happens in church life ceases to be intimately related to any or all
of these things, spirituality itself ceases, and peripheral piety begins. And then the people wonder what if anything at church
("the God-realm," as most people perceive their church affili-
ation and church activities) has to do with their lives. They
wonder consciously, or they wonder unconsciously, but they
wonder.

We need to begin with this wondering, hidden in the heart
of the thick of things. Everyone wonders, whatever their level
of church savvy or parish commitment. People without a working definition of spirituality wonder. People on the professional
team that works in the rectory wonder. Leaders of small groups
in your restructuring parish, who have been volunteering since
the days of the Catholic Family Movement, wonder. Fathers,
perhaps sometimes you too wonder. I know I do! Therefore,
PARISH ALIVE! offers a plunge into the middle of things for everyone who wonders, a plunge from wherever they stand, here and
now, down into the deeper depths.

For instance, many people in your parish are more or less
unfamiliar with the meaning of spirituality or its desirability
and availability for the average layperson. It is unlikely these
people would go outside their geographical parish boundaries
to find out its meaning. It is improbable that they would be
motivated to go to a retreat center such as ours in search

of something that they are unaware holds any relevance for them. For years, some have kindly inserted blurbs in parish bulletins, announcing retreats or courses to be presented at our center. The response from the general parish population has been slight; most people do not see such notices as intended for themselves. However, if I or another member of this team came to your parish on a Sunday evening, people could get a taste of wholistic spirituality, locally. It is my experience in parishes throughout New England and across the country that people's inner hungers remain unfed as long as these hungers remain unnamed; once people hear the words and experience the consonant reality that resonates within themselves, they seek more. As you glance again at our program, please notice the offering called "Spirituality for the Edge of an Age." It is geared for this general population and offers four generic topics for two-hour Sunday evening presentations in your parish: "All Called to Holiness," "Jesus, the Sacrament of the Father," "Praying the Seasons," and "Contemplative Prayer." Please feel free to list topics of your own choice that derive from these and may be particular to your own parish. Each topic adapts itself to a format that allows the participants an experiential dimension of prayer, ritual, interior and communal dialogue, as well as teaching input. Your parishioners, seated around tables together in their church hall, with coffee perking in their own parish kitchen, are likely to sense a challenge and an empowerment for their right-now lives of which they have been unaware.

On the other hand, Fathers, what of that loyal handful of folks in your parish who never refuse you that extra commitment when you ask. At this point, you've called them together again, those veterans of volunteerism, to serve on your councils, head up ministries, catechize the kids, or, in some cases, to lead small basic communities within the larger parish. Some of you have been able to send these people to training seminars for a few sessions of "how-to," or to an enrichment conference once a year. Others, unfortunately, have had to begin unprepared, fuelled primarily by their typical generosity and goodness of heart. All of you, I know, feel in your bones that the parish cannot and should not operate at all, these days, without peer ministry among the parishioners, and all of you see inherent weaknesses as well as strengths in that situation. The strengths are obvious as so many nonordained people begin to claim the power of their baptism and the gifts of God's spirit within them to build up the body of Christ. But the major weakness is obvious too; in these days when the local parish is replacing the seminary as the training ground for ministry, who really is ministering to the lay ministers in the area of spirituality formation? Competence is a contemporary hallmark of ministry, competence that is not limited to functional competence, although that ability is an absolute requisite. Spiritual competence, including facility for prayer and discernment, and the relational competence of how to be with others of differing gifts and faith levels are also essential if a parish lay leader is to be confident and successful.

Marks of this threefold competency for ministry (spiritual, functional, and relational competency) include the capacity for adjusting expectations to the reality at hand, potential to disciple others for leadership roles, skillful and compassionate ability to companion peers one on one, on their own spiritual journeys. This profile of a small-group parish leader is preferable, I'm certain you agree, to the image of the harassed volunteer, manual in one hand, lists of telephone numbers of possible conscriptees in the other, with his or her frustration and stress levels rising higher, ever higher. For these folks, PARISH ALIVE! offers "Greater Things Than I Shall You Do," a three-track experience designed to help develop a spirituality of competency for lay parish leaders. Each track includes five to ten sessions that deal with topics from "Individual and Corporate Faith Development Stages" to "Role Play for Spiritual Companioning." The three tracks are spread over a year and a half, and each builds on the one before. Again, as in "...Edge of an Age," the emphasis is on experiential spirituality. The participants' growing awareness and development of their personal and communal spirituality are in the foreground rather

than purely academic or instructional sessions. Since participants in "Greater Things..." come from a number of parishes,
sessions are held at the center, and later in central parish lo-
cations. There is a collegial dimension to this process; it is
preferable that more than one leader come from each parish.
As small groups, they will enrich other small groups with their
unique stories and experience. We, on the center's team, as
professional spiritual directors, seek to empower lay leaders on
the local level to create spirituality centers within the ongoing
life of their own home parishes.

I continued to outline briefly the other offerings of PARISH ALIVE!
for the pastors. I told them about "Seasons of Celebration,"
weekend retreats at the center for groups of parishioners across
parish lines. These retreats would take place and be based on
the natural flow of spirituality centered on creation across the
four seasons; they would draw their energy from the Thomist
principle that "grace builds on nature." Pastors were impressed
that one of their number had already agreed to pay half of the
weekend's cost for any of his parishioners who would like to
attend such a retreat. Later in the evening, two others quietly
offered to follow suit; they saw possibilities, they said, for ministry groups or councils within their parishes to come to one of
these retreats together and expand their bonds of community.
Since this was the very root idea of the retreats, I was pleased.

I also described "Come Aside and Rest Awhile," Sunday afternoons of spirituality to be offered monthly at the center,
mini-versions of the seasonal retreats, for those parishioners
who might just want "a little more." Topics ranged from "Living
in a *Lumen Gentium* Church" and "A New Look at Reconciliation" to "The Rosary as Contemplative Prayer." The central
premise of these afternoons was to bring forth from the store-
house treasures of spirituality both old and new. Again, I
underlined that the experiential dimension would be empha-
sized and balanced with the instructional input.

And Fathers, I asked, what about your own ongoing spiritual

growth, together with your parish staff? For this need, PARISH
ALIVE! offers "One in Mind and Heart," which includes days of
reflection or series of consultations for priests and their staff
either at the center or in the parish. PARISH ALIVE! seeks to
touch into every level of parish life and development.

Hands shot up; voices called out. "This will take years!"
"I can see my average parishioner being willing to come to a
Sunday night talk...but a weekend, or a three-track thing? He
won't be ready for that for a couple of years down the line."
"Look at the dates for all these offerings...too ambitious...do
you really expect people to sign up for a weekend, when all they
thought they were getting into was a two-hour talk?" "Maybe
new leaders will surface from the Sunday night talks...but not
this year."

I suddenly realized that our guests were listening to all this
in a linear single dimension. The pastors saw before them a
"program" that cried out for accomplishment in one calendar
year, yet another noble experiment in blitz renewal, wherein
their whole parish was perceived as a single unit to be moved
within a given time from here to there.

No, I repeated, this is not a program; it is a process, an
attitude, a reimaging. All these offerings are available simultaneously to meet the needs of individual people, not the needs of
an organization. Some nodded recognition. Others still looked
puzzled. One pastor repeated his observation with a single word
change, that it would take years for his parish to be ready to
move through such a "process" from beginning to end.

I looked him in the eye. Father, I suggested, picture a big
glass bowl containing a green jello dessert. The top layer is
plain lime jello, the next layer is pale and creamy whipped jello,
the next layer is clear jello and contains mixed fruit. One dessert, many layers...your spoon cuts through them all...you
taste them all in one cool bite. "Ahhh," he said. "I see."

This exchange reminded me of exactly how powerful and
entrenched is the traditional image of parish; parish as a
self-contained, homogeneous unit, a collective individual, an
entity with the single face of St. Someone's. The control-

ling image so mediates against the perception of a variety of unique persons with their individual needs and gifts and against the emerging hallmark of our own postmodern times, that of individual human transformation. It is no wonder that parochial life is moribund, or at least irrelevant in so many places.

The vicar and the coordinator each said a few supportive words. It was obvious that the pastors were surprised and favorably impressed that PARISH ALIVE! was happening with diocesan blessing and collaboration. Someone asked again, "Where do you suggest we begin?" Begin, I said, by signing your parish up for one or more of the twenty-four "Edge of an Age" Sunday evenings. Give some of your people an opportunity to experience the present-moment relevance of spirituality. Pastors murmured about going home to check parish calendars. But before they said goodnight, one of their number, the dean of a twenty-two-parish city deanery, asked me to give the same presentation to his next deanery meeting; in fact, he was willing to change the meeting date to accommodate my schedule. Others said they had had a wonderful time and would be in touch.

They had come; they had seen. I wondered.

Within the next two weeks, they called back. Over half the Sunday evenings we were offering for the next year were booked in that brief period. Three pastors offered financial backing for their leaders who would choose to attend the "Seasons of Celebration" retreats or the three-track "Greater Things" course. Two pastors who hadn't made the dinner made appointments to come and see me to get filled in. The dean sent me a copy of the letter he had sent to his twenty-two area pastors asking them to change the deanery meeting date on their calendars so that they could hear about PARISH ALIVE!. The coordinator of parish renewal made plans for me to come to speak to her Parish Alliance meeting, where small-group leaders of the restructuring parishes would be able to come in touch with PARISH ALIVE! All this and more took place before PARISH ALIVE! was one month old.

I stopped wondering. It was time for working. PARISH ALIVE!, I knew, was an idea whose time had come, whose reality needed to be seen. I invite you to sit down at table with me, to come and see what happened next, in the parish hall.

· 3 ·

SPIRITUALITY FOR THE EDGE
OF AN AGE

SCENARIO 1

What do the swirling galaxies have in common with the lower
church hall at St. T's-in-the-City? Everything and nothing! After all, the place is cavernous, and it *is* chilly down there in
the late autumn; the lights *are* there, but they have only two
settings, brilliant or brownout. Whereas the place is about as
aesthetically appealing as a black hole, it just doesn't have the
feel of a locale for the "cutting edge."

St. T's pastor had asked me to come and present a two-
hour session, "All Called to Holiness," on a Sunday evening in
mid-November. His parish is known throughout the diocese for
its superb liturgy; however, he worries about the depth-level of
spirituality and the degree of commitment to community that
must be foundational to the integrity of the assembly's liturgical prayer. And so he hoped that out of the "All Called" some
might respond to this invitation to seek more life.

Roundtables were set up; at each place was a harvest orange
sheet of paper featuring a picture of the earth and the notation
that the poem to be read as a basis of the evening's presentation would be, "Teach Us Your Ways, Lord" from *Guerillas of
Grace* by Ted Loder. One absolute principle undergirds PARISH
ALIVE!, that there are *no absolutes* other than God's presence
and love in the midst of God's people; there are no absolutely
foolproof methodologies, materials, or mechanism-miracles. On

41

the contrary, there is now developing an extraordinary and diverse body of spirituality resources in print and video, in poetry and prose. The classics are being retold, the present and future revisioned. Electronic instructors in sound spiritual principles, a myriad of minstrels and actors on God's video and audio stage such as Michael Sparough, SJ, new cosmologists like Thomas Berry discussing the mysterious interface of the physical universe and its triune Creator, prizewinning films like *Babette's Feast*, which move the viewer to examine human life as a sacred art — all these and many more are available to St. T's and the VCR in your own parish hall. You don't have to be harnessed by the busy lecture schedule of the "experts" or the "enrichment budget" of a depleted parish purse. Above all your attitude toward spiritual enrichment can shift from the one-dimensional packet program approach or the "perfect" (read no fee or stipend for this guru required!) on-site teacher paradigm, to the "potpourri of genius" pattern, available through steadily multiplying sources, as well as free or nearly so from your local diocesan resource center. (A partial listing of such resources is noted by chapter at the end of this book.) Our parochial limitations as centers of spirituality are narrowed only by the operative degree of our resourceful imaginations.

Back at St. T's on Sunday evening, I was the live and limited resource, but I saw the sixty people who came trickling in as the consciousness of the cosmos. As these parishioners, willing to come to church twice on one weekend, assembled with some hesitation at tables for eight, I reflected that there was more power here in the basement than in the weaponry of our most recent "small war." Here was the glory of God rising up to meet me, human beings desiring to be more fully alive. In all creation, only human consciousness is self-reflective; only human beings are conscious co-creators of cosmos out of chaos. It is ritual rather than rhetoric that can begin to provide an experiential consciousness of this self-identification for the participants.

And so we entered into that evening's ritual together, with a basic symbol of identity that everyone could recognize. I had

set a large crystal bowl of water on a small table at the front
of the room; a candle flickered beside it, and a strange unex-
plained piece of stone masonry lay in front of the bowl. We
began by listening to and then singing "Song over the Waters"
by Marty Haugen: "God, you have moved upon the waters, you
have sung in the rush of wind and flame: and in your love, you
have called us sons and daughters, make us people of the water
and your name."[1] A short meditation excerpted from *Woman-
Prayer, WomanSong* and *More Than Words: Prayer and Ritual
for Inclusive Community* was read, recalling the truth that the
same Spirit that moved over the primal chaos, the same Ruah
or breath of God, is present in each of us through the waters
of our baptism. Verses of the meditation were interspersed with
the repeated refrain from "Song over the Waters" until that music became a mantra of the tides of life within us. Then I called
upon the people to claim the power of their own baptism, as I
plunged my hands deep into the water, lifting it high, allowing
the water to run down my arms, the sound of its splashing recalling memories of our watery birth. I anointed all my senses,
eyes, mouth, head, hands, feet, and heart, each with a prayer
of claiming the power that is my birthright to free these senses
of mine to be further opened to receive God's presence, and to
mediate that presence to the world in which I live and move.
Finally, I anointed another with the water of power reclaimed,
by laying my hands upon the head of a surprised woman in
the first row. As the watery music continued to play, I invited
all those present to come to the water and also dare to claim
the power of their baptism. I asked them to freely plunge their
hands into the water, to feel its cooling touch, to anoint that
sense of their own most in need of freeing, and to choose to
anoint another person. Surely, the angel of God was stirring the
waters, for by ritual's end, as we sang the final refrain together,
there was a pregnant stillness that had fallen upon the room,
a yearning for the possibility of birthing.

　　Birthing of awareness of that which is really real is the foundational point of transformative spirituality. It has not so much
to do with *doing* as with *being*. Therefore, I explained that

since we were talking that evening on an ontological level, a place of mystery, the language of symbol inherent in poetry was a good place to begun. As I read Loder's poem "Teach Me Your Ways," all present focused on the earth picture, and we extrapolated three vital questions: Where are we? Who are we? What are we to become?

The prayer-poem's opening imagery evokes the Genesis mystery of the Spirit of God moving over the face of primordial chaos and identifies this Ruah with the Holy Spirit enlivening each of us, here and now in our own chaotic moment in history. The chaos or crisis of our times, when institutions and taken-for-granted securities seem to shatter even as we strive to protect them, can be seen as grace. If we examine the Chinese word for crisis, *wei chi*, we see that the first of the symbols that constitute that word means danger, beware; but the second means opportunity. Only when the ground of our personal beings, and our corporate being as society and as church, is shaken and stirred is there impetus for fundamental change and for growth in new directions. During historical periods of status quo maintenance, there may be a more "comfortable" stance toward life, but there is also little rationale for challenge or for exploration beyond present limits; the realm of mystery, of the treasure hidden deep in the dark underground of the field of our being may remain unfound.

We look again at the picture of earth in space, a picture that lived only in imaginal realms until our own lifetime when voyagers to the moon took with them the whole of human consciousness and focused back with their cameras to view the perfect simplicity and beauty of the world they had jumped free of. In that glance at our time and space reality from a first-time-in-human-history perspective, the pattern of human thought changed forever, as did the understanding of the scope of our Christian mission. In the generation since that shutter clicked, revealing a world too compact, too dependent on its wholeness and oneness for survival to admit of division, enormous advances in instant worldwide communication have been made just as vast chasms in interdisciplinary thinking and

cooperation have been bridged. There is a groaning toward oneness rising from the planet earth and reaching toward the stars
that have sung of wholeness for all the aeons of creation.

At this point in the presentation, I picked up the piece of
stone masonry from the table. It is a fist-sized fragment of the
Berlin wall that my oldest daughter had recently sent me as a
memento of her travels through eastern Europe. Affixed to its
surface is a dried flower that she found growing up through the
rubble of the destroyed wall and the collapsed system that the
wall represented. Out of chaos springs new life, tender, humble,
undefeatable. I asked the assembly, most of them near or over
forty years old, if they had ever expected to see that wall or that
system crumble in their lifetime. No! Most definitely not, they
answered, although they remembered praying for that dream as
children at the Latin Mass. One man objected that this "good"
news was really not so good; after all, a year had gone by since
that first rush to freedom and unity in Berlin, and now look at
all the problems in the Eastern bloc, the fighting, the renewed
attempts at repression. Birth is not easy, I reminded him; sometimes the struggle of labor is longer and harder than a woman
expects it to be, but once begun, the completion of the process
is already present in potential.

I continued to examine the question "Where are we?" as I
recounted the events of a limited analogy, a parallel in history
with which everyone was familiar, the Copernican revolution.
As long as the earth was the accepted center of the universe,
there were immutable laws of science and society, anchored in
that supposed centrality and founded in immutable but limited
images of God. Nicholas Copernicus challenged not only a scientific "given," but, by association, constellations of "givens"
in every field of human endeavor and human relational existence. It is no wonder that violent cries of "heretic" rose up to
greet his discovery. After all, if church and state were to accept
the new cosmological story, their very persons and positions as
guardians of the accepted order of things would be foundation-
ally threatened. And so they bent and twisted and contorted
themselves into every possible gyration that could make the

old order continue to "fit." They tied themselves up in knots to maintain a worldview that they could handle and control, even when everything pointed to its demise. Eventually, after decades of struggle, condemnation of the truth and repressive punishment of the innocent, the revolution begun by Copernicus yielded a completely new paradigm or mega-pattern for Western thinking and being and endeavor. Such a cataclysmic series of events in human understanding has been called by some a paradigm shift. Many, in fact more and more, scholars in theology, physics, and social sciences believe that we are living today in a time of whole-pattern shift, even perhaps that we are entering a new axial period in human history wherein the dualisms, belief system competition, suppression of human freedoms in the political power game, opposition of science and religion, and so many other accepted/unacceptable marks of the modern age (post-1500) are dying.

"Where are we?" I ask again. "On the edge of an age." "What does this have to do with spirituality, with Christianity?" one woman asks. I remind her and all of us of the prayer of Jesus in John 17: "Father, may they all be one, even as you and I are one, so the world may know you sent me." I suggest that the planet earth and all its people have consciously and actively entered into that prayer; that our lived spirituality as Christian people has not only to do with a local dimension, but simultaneously with a global dimension, if it is to reflect "life in all its fullness" that Jesus claims is his gift to us (John 10:10). The assembly begins to see the large picture of earth from space that I have brought with me as a holy icon for our times, a representation of God's work of art; individuals begin to actively sense their own unavoidable connection to that "holy picture" and the personal implications for a shift in the "me and God" spirituality toward "God in all things, all things in God" model for Christians called to holiness at the edge of an age. They are sensing their personal responsibility in Christ to discover new images, newer, more wholistic realities, hidden within familiar and traditional terms.

Referring back to "Teach Me Your Ways," I began to approach the second of this evening's basic questions, "Who are we?" Loder's imagery quickens the awareness of life lived to the full across the spectrum of joy and pain. Am I my masks, my roles, my position, or am I a human being, created in God's image and likeness? Upon what image of God, inherent in our Tradition, can we all agree? This one, certainly: that God is Trinitarian. So I draw a triangle on the board provided for me, and label each corner, Father (Mother), Son, and Spirit. Of course, this is symbolspeak, and I do not expect to arrive in heaven to see and praise a golden triangle upon an ivory base. This triadic image is the representation of relationship, the Creator so loving the Word and the Son-Word so loving the Abba-Creator, and the Spirit being the Love that joins them, and all this being the action of loving in the total dynamic relationship of the Godhead. There is nothing static about this Trinitarian relationship; rather it is whirling and pulsing with an energy of love so infinitely creative that it spills over to be reflected in all of creation, which bears its stamp.

I erase one corner of the triangle on the board. What happens to the relationship, to the triadic image if one angle disappears? The whole thing collapses through disconnection comes the response. Yes, I reply, our God is dynamic relationship. And it follows that if we are made in the image of this God, as Genesis tells us, we must look like this too.

Jesus knew this and spoke it and lived it. When he was asked, for instance, for his consideration of the greatest commandment, the glue that holds the whole Law together, he replied that the first commandment is to love God with one's whole self, body, mind, spirit, and emotions; and the second is identical to and of equal value with the first, that is, to love others in the identical manner and intensity with which we love ourselves.

On the board, I draw another triangle and label the three angles God, Self, and Others. We human beings live in relationship to God, to others, and to our own self. Again, if I erase one corner, the image collapses through disconnection. Not a problem, we all say; I love God, I pray, I go to church, I contribute to the budget, I'm even a catechist! That's how much I love God, but the trouble is my rotten brother-in-law, Harry! I mean, how can I love that man? He has ruined every family gathering with his horrible personality and all his other unmentionable but glaring problems all these last twenty years! What? I have to love Harry if I claim to love God? Yes, as John asks in his first letter, "How can you claim to love God whom you can't see, if you do not love the brother whom you do see?" (1 John 4:20). Okay! Okay! I'll make an effort to love Harry, and I'll make extra efforts to love everyone else; why, I'll even beat myself into the ground loving the fools at the office and the kids as they demand their fifth ride of the day; I'll be the perfect mother, wife, cook, housecleaner, professional woman. When I sink into my bed at 2 A.M. after loving and doing for yet another nail-in-the-coffin kind of a day, I'll do so with the satisfaction that I'm fulfilling the great commandment!

Wait now, Jesus maintains that you are called to love others in the same measure and with the same quality that you love yourself! Which pole of the triadic image that is human relationship is the real beginning of all this, anyway? Very reluctantly, the gathered group admits it probably all starts with loving yourself. "That sounds so selfish!" One person says it, but many nod agreement. Could it be that we never followed Jesus' logic as we read his words on this issue? Could it be that our notion of humility, gathered through our years of schooling and inculturation, had nothing to do with its root word *humus*, that is, earth/dirt/reality; that we never actually knew to be humble means to be rooted to the earth, standing firmly in the truth of being who we are, that is, well-loved, worthy creatures?

Try this, I suggest: Remember back to early this morning when you stumbled into your bathroom and flicked on the wonderfully revelatory fluorescent lights. You picked up your toothbrush, your razor, your comb and looked straight into that mirror with the joyous greeting, "Hi, gorgeous! Hi, Handsome!" Laughter (somewhat raucous) explodes in the church basement. "No? You forgot to do that?" I ask innocently. Well, that's how our God wants each of us to view ourselves, as the beautiful, beloved one whom God's own Self imagined and brought into being. At least, that's Jesus' impression of the whole thing. And he had the ancient backing of Genesis, which tells us that God was mightily pleased, in fact in love with every aspect of the Creation. God saw what God had made and said, "Mmmm, that's good!"

Looking again at Jesus' lived out, enfleshed Trinitarian reflection, we can see the paschal mystery rising up in triadic image. The threefold reality of Jesus' incarnate being is life, death, and resurrection, the very same threefold pattern to which we who bear his name are called. The paschal mystery evaporates if any of its three poles disappears. Cycle upon cycle of our own lives imitates this Christic pattern. Oh, it's not our final inevitable dying that is the hardest, but rather the many deaths we suffer through loss, failure, disappointment, illness, dissolution of relationships. We cannot avoid or control our daily dyings; those little deaths enflesh the poverty of our human condition. In an earlier and distorted theology with which many of us grew up, these daily deaths, i.e., sufferings or crosses, were to be welcomed as sure signs of "holiness." In fact, if things were going well for you this year and God did not give you a current "cross" to bear, why not build one yourself? To be bowed down in suffering, good for its own sake, was the mark of a good Catholic. After all, if you just carried your cross long and painfully enough, Jesus would most certainly leap out of the hedges, where he was hidden somewhere down the road, to help you before it was too late and to assure you that you had "earned" heaven. Sound familiar?

I too used to think of the paschal mystery in my life (after I got over thinking of it as three days of churchgoing in March or April) in terms of linear time, cause and effect, "earning" salvation through suffering. I can recall a moment when all that changed for me some years ago; it was a very painful period in my life, dark with death and endings. I was making a retreat that summer in Gloucester, Massachusetts. As I sat that golden morning on a high cliff over the sun-dancing ocean, raspberry bushes heavy with fragrant fruit just behind me, I saw and experienced none of it. I was thoroughly blind to the beauty before me; in the inscape of my soul it was endless night. Idly, I flipped the pages of a book in my lap, mindlessly willing to endure yet another day of meaningless pain. And then, in a spare but light-blinding instant, these words leaped at my heart: *death is resurrection.*

My linear categories exploded in the flash of light and in the reassembled triadic image of my own grace-filled paschal mystery. I realized I had dragged my cross alone along a time line, every day of which urged me to evade, deny, not feel the pain, or else bear it stoically until the resurrection moment sometime in the future might magically cancel my debt. Now I suddenly saw that I had the freedom to choose to enter into the heart of my own human poverty, to embrace rather than strive to escape the darkness; then I would see and be embraced by the risen Christ who lives as a point of light in the very heart of the darkness itself. By yielding consciously to the present death rather than trying to avoid it, fix it, bargain with God about it, mindlessly bear it, I was already in possession of risen life. This risen life is a transformed, stretched, more deeply human life that I could not possibly experience while held prisoner by the crippling fear of losing the limited, "comfortable" life that had been. My eyes opened to the glorious dapple of sun on sea; I drank in the airborne flavor of the berries; I exalted in the love of the holy One who is always with me, in the midst of the mess!

Am I willing to live this triadic pattern of life, death, and resurrection over and over again, on deeper and deeper levels, so that I may experience the kingdom more fully in the here and now, this kingdom that is after all God's presence in human activity? Am I willing to accept the invitation to discipleship, to live in the pattern of the Master who emptied himself and became poor? Am I willing to become poor enough to be fully human — that is, to live to the outer reaches of experiential acknowledgment of creaturehood?

But how can we be said to be poor, how can we recognize

our poverty, we who live in this society? After all, we are the "haves," not the "have-nots." Our poverty is so easy to ignore what with our credit cards, houses, cars! Do you recall Teresa of Calcutta's comments on this subject, televised as she addressed the Harvard commencement some years ago? Smartly tailored men, jeweled women, gowned undergraduates, the leading lights of academia, all these were caught by the roving TV camera as their expressions became frightened and pained by the truth to which they listened and the empty echoes resonating within themselves. Teresa of Calcutta, that wizened disciple of Jesus Christ, that little, bent women in a worn sweater that was in such contrast to the regalia of the day, told the grand assemblage that the poverty she had seen in the West was so much deeper, so much more intensely sad than all the poverty of her India. There, she said, it was merely a hunger for bread, but here it is the starvation of loneliness, alienation, meaninglessness, lack of love.

Yes, we share the poverty of Jesus Christ, the poverty of being human, as long as we do not hide from its experience either by sublimation or stoicism. And if we do agree truly to live out our humanity, as he did, from the heights of joy to the depths of pain, in the awareness of the Spirit who enlivens and enables us, Loder's poem insists we will live as prophets in our time. Like the prophet Micah, we can say to one another, to our church and world, "This is what God requires of you, to live justly, to love tenderly, to walk humbly with your God" (Mic. 6:8). What is meant by living justly? Walter Brueggemann defines the scriptural notion of divinely mandated justice to the poor very simply: "To sort out what belongs to whom and to return it to them."[2] And just who is the "whom" calling out for our attention? In each of our lives, *whom* is God, myself, and others, and so we return to the Trinitarian image of God, and the lived-out likeness of that image that I greet each day in my early morning mirror.

"Teach Me Your Ways" images each of us as a steward and healer of the earth and all its creatures. "If anyone is in Christ, there is a new creation" (2 Cor. 5:17). Do you hear the invitation to behold yourself even as God beholds you? Can you imagine the self-imposed boundaries, shaped and limited at least in part by the society in which we all live, beginning to soften and melt? Can you further imagine those boundaries becoming so porous that you can see that all that is you is a vital and integral part of all that there is? As you would protect your own body from injury, can you imagine the same intimate interconnectivity and care between what you call *yourself*, and what you have been calling *other* than yourself, but which you can now begin to see as the corporate person to which you belong, the Body of Christ? Can you begin to extend this corporate image even further to a scale encompassing all creation, the Cosmic Christ? In what ways would this spirituality cause you to live differently? What if some others whom your life touches also began to imagine and live in this new way? What if many others, and finally all others, adopted this wider, deeper dimension of spirituality as their own? Yes, you can begin to see a transformed humanity, a flourishing earth. Teilhard de Chardin dreamed a similar dream as he envisioned all of creation charged through with divinity. He called his image the "divine milieu," and his work challenges individual Christian consciousnesses to become so transformed as to live toward absolute individual potential. You are called to continue the co-creation of the universe as it evolves toward the "Omega Point" wherein all things are willingly under the lordship of Jesus Christ. Your mission as Christians is cosmic.

Chapter 7 of *Lumen Gentium* (Vatican II, November 21, 1964), "The Pilgrim Church," called us to this eschatological awareness of the kingdom in the making and to our personal responsibility for bringing it forth. This greater birthing, as with all conception, begins with dreams for the future that seem impossible. But with Mary, first of the disciples, we can say, "With God, all things are possible" (Luke 1:8). "Who are we?" Yes, of course! We, like her, are first and foremost disciples.

≈

Energies were high and vital in the church basement. It was time for a refreshment break, but before we paused, I distributed rose-colored pamphlets for journaling. The front cover was a reprint from *Sundays Doorposts*, reproducible designs of Scripture quotations done in calligraphy by Timothy Botts. This one reads, "Nothing, nothing, nothing is impossible with God." I asked the group to return to their tables at break's end, to expect meditative instrumental music, and there prayerfully to consider themselves, the world, and the church twenty years from now and to dare to dream tonight of future realities they hoped to see actualized in any of those three spheres. I said they would have ten minutes for that interior consideration, ten additional minutes to journal their reflections in the pink booklets, and twenty additional minutes to express those dreams to the others at their tables.

Amazing opportunities arise at coffee breaks! A group of six St. T parishioners approached me as I stirred sugar into my coffee and introduced themselves as the newly constituted "spirituality committee" for the parish. They wondered if I had any ideas that might be helpful as they were starting to plan spiritual activities from point zero. Why, yes, I replied. Why not consider a weekend retreat at the center, or perhaps a ten-week course called "Greater Things Than I" to further equip yourselves for this ministry? "Oh, we're overcommitted already," they chorused. "Oh, no, I have young children." "Oh, no, what we meant is perhaps you have materials you could recommend." "Uh huh," I said, understanding immediately. (I want you to remember these six women. You'll meet them again in chapters 7 and 8. After all, nothing is impossible with God!).

I put a tape on the recorder, "Autumn" by George Winston, and invited all to return to their places. A hushed reverence softened the church basement as the sounds of the season that was also swirling outdoors anchored hearts to the present moment, the only place and time where a person can find the God who is. Soon people began to write their reflections, and they did so with determination and intensity although I was certain that the majority of those present was not accustomed to journaling as a way of prayer. I felt their palpable relief and release as they wrote, communicating their hearts' response. I lowered the music and invited all into dialogue at their respective tables. The talk flowed easily and immediately as each little cell of eight poured forth hopes and visions to friends and strangers.

As I walked quietly around the room, I saw some people reading their written reflections aloud, some listening deeply and attentively to others, some urgently sharing their thoughts on current pain and future hope. I saw and heard laughter and tears, longing and compassion, and, at every table, engagement in the dialogue. It was startling that in this parish the first formal attempt at small-group faith sharing was so rich. I saw the seeds of basic communities, wherein people would learn to break the bread of their lives together, planted that evening in the church basement. I felt the ease with which these parishioners and neighbors entered into the mystery of mutual vulnerability and knew that this modest event was answering a long-term hunger. I was touched to see the pastor telling his story with passion at the table he shared equally with seven other women and men. A song ran through my mind, a simple song that Mexican field workers sing as they walk on their way from several villages to a shared eucharistic celebration. Their lyrics rise to the morning sky, telling the tale that they join and go together to the table where there is a chair for everyone, the table where every brother, every sister, no matter how poor, has a mission and a position.

The sharing experience flowed easily back into the presentation, as we returned to "Teach Us Your Ways" where the poet speaks of the "ancient vision of mothers" that can flame within me and ignite and give warmth to a waiting humankind. I spoke of the vision, appealing to the parents in the room, reminding them to recall the birth of their firstborns. The pain was immense, perhaps, but it vanished when at last they held that tiny one in their hands and saw a brand new face of God. Each of us, as disciple, is being born as we enter the process of interiority, community, and transformation. As hard a struggle as it is, we don't have to be born alone. We move into that new life together.

What is that new life? "What are we to become?" Haven't we already answered that question as we considered discipleship, as we asked where and who we are? As we become experientially conscious of ourselves as disciples of Jesus in this time and place, and as we live imperceptibly into our understanding of what this really means, we become fully human, fully alive, capable of lighting the world. We become the Transfiguration! Scriptural scholars tend to agree that what Peter, James, and John saw on Mt. Tabor, the hill of Jesus' transfiguration, was not his divinity. No, we cannot see the face of God unveiled and live. What they saw was the fullness of Jesus' humanity, and it was so startling, so magnificent that they desired to remain there, in that moment of revelation, forever. But you remember the story. They had to walk away from that instant of glory, return to the town from which they came, and personally live into that glory themselves. Transfiguration was to be their own destiny and ours.

I invited the group to reflect on Peter's own living memory of the event of Jesus' transfiguration, when he, Peter, was older and wiser: "...take it [this memory] as a lamp for lighting a way through the dark until the dawn comes and the morning star rises in your minds" (2 Pet. 1:16–19). I shared a poem that I had written some years before to celebrate the Feast of the Transfiguration. The three disciples are much older now, and James is speaking to John....

UNTIL THE MORNING STAR[3]

Sometimes I look at you and still see
Tabor-light rising in your eyes.
It's been so many mountain roads
for Peter, you and I, my friend.

Have the night sea journeys troubled you as
well as me? Have you called our names
and His? — "When again? Tell me when
the cloud will cover us, the voice of God again
     enflame
our flesh, our very ordinary hearts?" A part
of me grieves on forever for the moment gone....
I often wonder why we could not build those tents,
spend all our lives upon that holy hill?
So many years have passed — and still
this old man's dreams remember, weep and wait.

And lately, John, even when I wake from dreams,
it seems that all I see is Him — everywhere,
in every face and place I pass — Beloved One,
shining Son, setting fire to the dimness of the days,
making bright the darkest corners, bringing light
to thickest nights, and breadth to narrow ways....

The shapes and colors I have known are melting,
changing, swirling in the dawn — growing violent,
     vibrant
swelling into song — and I am leaping like a young
     man —
dancing altogether up the mountain toward home.

We closed our evening by playing the tape "Servant Song"
by Rory Cooney and singing it together, "This is my servant
whom I shall I uphold, his name is Christ is her name!"[4] Yes!
We are to be transfigured; *we* are to become the Christ!

Before saying goodnight to the people of St. T's, I told them
I would be back the following week, at their pastor's request, to
speak to their parish ministry council members and give them
further information and invitation to PARISH ALIVE! As the year
unfolded, St. T's would opt for full and fruitful participation in
the process.

SCENARIO 2

Fifteen miles north of the center, driving along coastal 1A, you approach a charming village founded early in the eighteenth century. On a December evening, white lights twinkle from every ancient tree in town and dance in the windows of each unique shop and venerable plaque house along Main Street. Solstice magic pirouettes with the first lacy snowflakes of another winter. Down at the harbor, visible behind the houses, some boat owners have trimmed sailless masts in the white lights (the only glitter allowed in this proud traditional village) to create the illusion of waterborne Christmas trees. And the stars go on dancing their pre-Christmas ballet in the frosty black sky over St. P's Episcopal Church right in the center of town.

Two couples, active members of St. P's, who were participating in programs at the center, had approached me in the early fall. Little yellow brochures in hand, they had asked, "Is this PARISH ALIVE! thing for Roman Catholics only? It looks like just what we've been waiting for at St. P's!" I replied that it would be a delight for me to spend a Sunday evening at St. P's, and perhaps, after discussion with their rector, they might get back to me with a date during Advent, since their topic of choice was "Praying the Seasons" (for an expanded answer to my friends' question, please see Appendix 1, which deals with ecumenical implications for PARISH ALIVE!).

Arrangements had been made immediately, as well as details agreed upon for a brief article concerning PARISH ALIVE! and the resources of the center in *South County Churchman*, a local newsletter of the Episcopal diocese. So it was that I placed my dried flower Advent wreath and in its center my Haitian woodcarving of an evocative pregnant Mary on a small antique table to set the mood in the chapter room at St. P's on the first Sunday evening of Advent. The newly designed chapter room itself, with its high windows, long narrow floor plan, warm wood tones and sconces on the walls to further soften recessed track lighting, gave visible witness to the blend

of venerable past and contemporaneity that the Tradition of this
church espouses.

The Thomist maxim that "grace builds on nature" would
be the core principle tonight as we would strive to evoke past,
present, and future. Liturgical seasons make sense only when
they are sensibly celebrated, that is, celebrated with reverence
for all the human senses, physical, intellectual, and spiritual.
In fact, my understanding of wholistic spirituality in general,
has that sensible notion as its foundation. Wholistic spirituality is like a full-bodied wine. It is a stance toward God, self,
and the community that takes into account the rich flavors and
nuanced fragrances of what it means to be a human being, the
memories, conscious and unconscious, of personal and communal beginnings and growth, the creative artistry with which the
sanctity of life itself is appreciated and presented, the mellow
and perfect complementarity that the interior spiritual journey
has with existent, external reality, the longing for more.

Our opening prayer and ritual began by candlelight as we
listened to a taped song, "Each winter as the year grows older,
we each grow older too; the cold sets in a little colder; the verities we knew seem shaken and untrue."[5] The plaintive melody
touched into the real-life wintry situations of many of the forty
people gathered there, as did the hope of the final verse: "Yet
I believe beyond believing, that life shall spring from death;
that hope shall flower in our grieving; that we shall catch
our breath, and turn, transfixed by faith." In the poignant atmosphere that linked us to all human generations waiting in
winter for the sun (the Son) to return, George Winston's piano
composition "December" began to play. Snatches of childhood
Christmas memories are subtly woven with his music.

The music softened and I asked the assembly to close their
eyes, to rest their hands on their laps, to sit comfortably with
backs straight and legs and feet uncrossed. I asked them to
notice their breathing, to breathe in the presence of God, to
breathe out the tensions they might notice in various parts of
their bodies, and with those tensions, their inner anxieties. So
centered, they entered a receptive state of inner listening to the

guided imagery meditation that I spoke. I asked them to travel deeply, down into the past, to a now faraway December when they were small. I suggested sounds, scenes, feelings of their personal long agos. When I asked them to picture those gathered with them, or those sadly absent in their distant but still so present memories, a deep sense of love-experienced rested on the room. Like a ribbon of memories, those realities, still very much alive in their hearts' imagination, unwound and linked all that once was to the now of this particular Advent.

When the words of the meditation ended, the reality of bringing the past into the present prevailed, as the rector read for us from the day's first reading: "Oh, that you would rend the heavens and come down..." (Isa. 6:4). We responded with "Psalm of an Emerging Emmanuel" by Edward Hays from *Prayers for a Planetary Pilgrim*, five people reading the consecutive verses. Then, as I turned up the music of "December," I spread a long ivory ribbon, flowered in wintry colors, in front of the Advent wreath, the ribbon's edges trailing town the sides of the table. I invited the participants to recall those special persons with whom they had had interior communion during the guided meditation, those people who in one way or another gave birth to the men and women they are today, and to come forward and write the names of these members of their personal communion of saints on the ivory ribbon with markers I provided. (I had heard from my four friends who initiated this evening that their congregation was fairly conservative about prayer and ritual so I had better be cautious about asking them to do anything new or different; they simply would refuse to enter in!) Every person in the room rose and came forward, some with tears glistening in their eyes or unabashedly rolling down their cheeks. We ended with a gathering prayer pointing toward our boundless future birthed with Emmanuel, God With Us, here in our winter midst.

The presentation itself opened with a choice and a challenge. We might opt to *ignore* the season of Advent with the rest of our culture for whom Christmas begins as Halloween ends; or we might opt to *celebrate* the season that implies a

wholesome, folksy, household keeping of St. Nicholas candy
cane day, St. Lucy's candle-crowned morning, Advent calendar on the refrigerator, Advent wreath on the supper table. And
these are good things to do, mind you. Or we might plunge into
mystery and actually *pray* the season of Advent. If we choose
to pray the season, we are challenged to discover an image,
words, and an experience.

An image: A poor little dark man named Luis carved the
Mary who stands at the center of our Advent wreath; he carved
her slender and faceless from a single piece of smooth wood.
Her face is tilted, looking down upon the infant head resting
under her chin and yet her belly is still great with child. Third
world theology at its best! As we look we might see her and
ourselves, having given birth but still pregnant with waiting for
so much more; we might see the already but not yet of the
kingdom.

Words: The Cycle B readings, common to both Episco-
palian and Roman Catholic lectionaries this Advent, speak
cogently each week of waiting, watchfulness, and being wonder-
full. They speak of longing, being and becoming. They speak
of gift and grace too marvelous to anticipate, but anticipated
nonetheless. They speak and speak and speak to us of new
birth.

An experience: Pregnancy is an experience with which we
are all familiar. Even if we have not mothered or fathered a
child ourselves, we have been near someone who has. Most
fundamentally of all, each of us has spent the first part of our
own human lives in the symbiotic life-flow of the womb. If indeed we have waited for a child, we recall in our flesh and our
bones the trimesters of pregnancy. We learned to wait, to watch,
and finally to be wonder-full. We experienced the long waiting
for the invisible process to unfold, we already loved the newly
forming individual self, distinct from our own self, but still perceived as part of us. We learned to be watchful as we saw our
bodies change, noticed the accommodations in our own schedules and activities and anticipated the very different pattern of
life to which we would adapt in the not too distant future when

the child would be born. At last, after long-focused attention to the invisible, unknown little one, there he or she was, held to our breasts and we wept, and laughed with the surprise and wonder of this tiny, sacred revelation of divine love.

I suggested that in this context of image, words, and experience we look at Advent from the threefold perspective of Bernard of Clairvaux, who maintained that there are really three Advents. The first is Bethlehem and exists in the past; the third is the moment when Jesus will come in glory, fulfilling the parousia, and that is in an undetermined future. It is the middle Advent that needs to be addressed, and that is the coming of Christ into our lives, now in this present moment. Perhaps we could line up the trimesters of pregnancy, the actions of waiting, watching, and being wonder-full, the past, present, and future, with Bernard's three Advents as we enter the prayer that is this season.

Advent time is, of its nature, for remembering and for storytelling. The remembering goes beyond our personal history; we recall echoes of our corporate memory as the centuries-old people of God. There are hidden treasures and gifts of truth and illumination ready to be unwrapped in the spiral of every age that has led to our own. I use three selections from the thirteenth-century Rhineland mystic Meister Eckhart to punctuate the three segments of my presentation. These verses point to the three action phases of pregnancy and announce the birthing of Christ in a new way in our own lives.

As we "wait" in the darkness following the conception of deeper relationship with God, we need only breathe "yes." I tell stories of real people who wait in the darkness, pregnant with God's call and promise; the story of a Jesuit friend making his final vows today, speaking his deeply discerned "yes," about to leave a successful fifteen-year artistic career to devote an undetermined number of years to service in the third world because he feels called to a place where he can learn what only the poor can teach him. And I tell the story of a black permanent deacon in a southern Catholic church who, with the rest of his parish, has waited for decades for a pastor personally connected to the culture he serves. While he waits, he tells warm and hilarious stories of the outrageous mismatches that have become standard and only serve to bring his people closer to the faithful "yes" of waiting that God requires.

As we "watch" for Christ who comes in the ordinary flesh of men and women, we become more and more alert to the promise of metanoia. I tell the story of a religious sister in her mid-fifties who is steeped in outraged anger at an in-law whom she judges has been unfaithful to one of her family members. But as she watches the screen of her own memories, she recalls a poignant incident that occurred in her early twenties, in the winter twilight of the seamiest section of a big Eastern city. Hurrying along with friends, for a brief moment her eyes had locked with those of another unknown young woman. She remembers being struck by the loveliness of the other's face and being certain that here indeed was a counterpart of young Mary of Nazareth. This urban "Mary" gazed at her with wonder and simplicity. The two of them had become one in shared humanity and compassion. The young sister, in full traditional habit, suddenly noticed that the other was dressed in the net stockings, spiky heels, and slinky skirt that spoke of her profession. And yet deep had called unto deep from one pair of a "stranger's" eyes to the other. Now, in this day thirty years later, the sister weeps with newborn compassion for the "immoral" person she has lately judged. Compassion feels from the depths the pain and brokenness of another. Next Sunday, the second of Advent, we will listen to Isaiah's fortieth chapter, where God promises that if the people will watch for the promised One, they will see every valley lifted up and every mountain and hill made low (Isa. 40:4). Can we imagine that these mountains and valleys are the arrogant and empty places of our own hearts?

Can we also be watchful like that great wild Advent-man, John the Baptist? John's story of watchfulness (Matt. 11:2–11) is included in the Cycle A Advent readings. Not so long ago, a friend of mine, an excellent homilist, based his preaching that third Cycle C Advent Sunday on the question the Baptist sent to Jesus from prison: "Are you the one who is to come or are we to look for another?" He was aware he had done a brilliant job with the text, even before parishioners pumped his hand at the door thanking him for his insightful and inspired words. Later that week, Father attended the wake of a parishioner, whose wife he had ministered to as she faced the sudden death of her husband. She was seated in the receiving line, unable to rise through her black grief, so he knelt to tell her of his sorrow and to add that he would be unable to celebrate the requiem Mass, as he had a previous commitment of long duration in a distant city on the same day as the funeral; he was to give a talk for a large and distinguished gathering. She said nothing, only gazed at him long and painfully. Her eyes screamed out to his breaking heart, "Are you the one who is to come, or shall I look for another?" (Luke 7:18–20). The priest cancelled his travel plans; he was there for the bent-over woman; the word was made flesh.

Meister Eckhart wrote that the Creator extends to us the power of divine incarnation, the same power that brought forth the firstborn Child of the Creator: " ... extends this same power to you out of the divine maternity bed located in the God-head to eternally give birth."[6] What an ecstatic surprise it is to find that we ourselves are the extension of the Incarnation! We are wonder-full and wordless as we discover that truth on deeper and deeper yet ordinary levels. Wonder-full surprise is the final aspect of the Advent birthing process. I am lifted to extra-ordinary heights as I receive the gift of myself, the poor little one transformed.

Once, pregnant with my fourth daughter and just recovering from a serious bout with pneumonia, I sat alone in my kitchen, peeling shrimp on a Christmas Eve afternoon. The other three children were out with their dad, attending to last minute shopping; I sat there lonely, heavy, still somewhat ill and feeling incredibly sorry for myself. When the doorbell rang, I came close to panic; I was too much of a mess to accept a holiday visit. However, there was nothing else to do but dry my eyes with the fishy dishtowel and open the door. There stood the surprise visitor, the Cistercian priest who acted as my spiritual director. He had driven a long way on this busy day to arrive at my door with a large, mysterious green book under his arm. He said, "If I were your father (my own German father had been dead for many years) and I knew my 'baby' (the name my father always called me) was having a baby and not feeling well, I would have come to visit her this afternoon." He walked to the Christmas tree, opened the music book he carried, and in his melodic voice, beautifully practiced in the monastic choir, he sang "O Tannenbaum," all its verses, in German. Then he asked if he could bless the baby, and laying his hand on my abdomen, with the child still jumping all about to the Christmas music, he prayed for a safe delivery. He said quietly as he moved to leave when the prayer ended, "This is Bethlehem." The surprise Christmas Eve visit had lasted under fifteen minutes but my being and my world were transformed. It was Christmas; I was a loved daughter of my Father in heaven. I was wonder-full!

The folks in the chapter room were wide-eyed as any children at story hour as their own stories connected with those that I had told. Story was Jesus' own medium for teaching basic truths, story wherein the human condition is raw material for birthing the divine. In agreement with Pope Paul VI's oft-quoted comment that the world doesn't often listen to teachers anymore, and if it does, it listens only to those teachers who witness (tell stories), the incarnational spirituality espoused by PARISH ALIVE! has much to do with storytelling. Use your own stories, get permission to use your friends' stories, read stories like John Shea's *Stories of God* and the wonderful stories collected by Anthony De Mello in *Song of the Bird*, but do remember to teach as Jesus taught, that master of parable and story!

After a hot chocolate break, St. P's people had an opportunity to listen to a bit more of Winston's "December" as they considered their own currently developing stories of birthing the Christ in this time and place. They too had received journaling booklets, covers covered in stars and quoting Isaiah 40:26: "Lift

your eyes and look to the heavens: Who created all these? The
one who brings out the starry host one by one, and calls them
each by name." The reflection question I offered was this: As
you imagine the Christmas star rising over your personal Bethlehem this year, in what new way are you called to allow Christ
to be born of you? There was sharing and mutual reflection and
we closed with music, "A Time Will Come for Singing" from
Gentle Night by the St. Louis Jesuits.

One of the parish priests present that evening told my
friends a few days later that the "Edge of an Age" talk on
Sunday was the first time in his life he had ever considered
himself to be pregnant, and pregnant with God. He said he
had much to pray about and that his Advent and Christmas would be deeper somehow this year. A number of people
from St. P's congregation accepted my invitation to the weekly
Advent mornings at the center and returned in the spring
for weekly Lenten mornings. A core group planned to regis-
ter for the three-track "Greater Things..." offering, to prepare
themselves to lead groups of other congregants in ongoing
spirituality and faith-sharing groups. PARISH ALIVE! is for people.

SCENARIO 3

Well before the New Year announced itself, news of PARISH
ALIVE! had spread beyond the original ten pastors and their
parishes. An assistant pastor from a sprawling northern Rhode
Island parish, with whom I had worked some years before on
the Providence Vocation Council, called the center in late winter. He asked if I could give four April Sunday evenings at his
church. He added that they'd take all four "Spirituality at the
Edge of an Age" topics because they had a sizable "spirituality
budget" and hadn't known quite what to do with it until he
heard from fellow priests about PARISH ALIVE! Fr. Bob Caul, my
colleague on the team at the center, and I had split the twenty-
four Sunday evening presentations according to our schedules
and we agreed we could manage two more a piece.

On the last Sunday in April I headed for 295 North, and in under an hour a springtime ride in lengthening light brought me to O.L. Parish and a presentation on "Contemplative Prayer." I wondered if it was the unseasonably warm weather that had limited the size of this group to twenty. I had wondered at St. M's in mid-state last Sunday too, during a raging thunderstorm where I had gone to present the same topic. Or could it be that "contemplative prayer" itself has a threatening ring to all but would-be Carmelites? Before we began, I asked the folks for their definitions of contemplation. Answers ranged from "what the monks do" to "hypnotic trance" to a "gift for saints." Sublime encouragement! Ministry *must* meet pastoral needs, and the need for understanding and especially for experiencing the buried treasure of contemplation is paramount in today's Catholic Church.

I had divided this evening into three parts, the first, centering prayer, and third, *lectio divina*, would be experiential; the second would be a history lesson. We gathered around a tall white Christ candle as I described the elements of centering prayer based on Thomas Keating's summary in chapter 10 of his book *Open Mind, Open Heart: The Contemplative Dimension of the Gospels.* Only two people in the room were familiar with the term "centering prayer"; no one claimed to have had experienced it. I began the prayer experience by reading a prayer of Elizabeth of the Trinity, and I told the group that a chant would be played, based on that prayer, continuously for the seven or eight minutes that followed. The chant by Gerald May is found on *Sound Faith* and was recorded by the Shalem Institute in the Joseph of Arimathea chapel below the main altar of the National Cathedral in Washington, D.C. The sound therefore echoes in the depths and blends with the natural rhythm of a slowed heart beat: "Changeless and calm, deep mystery. Ever more deeply rooted in Thee."[7] The chant would serve as a mantra, a sacred word on which they could travel down along the interior river of their own beings, past thoughts and emotions to the still point source-place where God's own Spirit dwells with their own. Once there, they would not do or say or expect anything, except to be with God.

A single bell-silver note ended the mantra and I gently drew the people back up from their inward journey with a shared "Our Father." I asked several questions: "How did your body feel during the prayer? Your mind? Were you able to flow with the sacred word to your deep self? Were you comfortable or uncomfortable with the process? Why? Can you sum up your experience with one sentence?" The answers reflected a wide variety of experience, but two remarks were constants: "I didn't believe anything would happen, but it did!" and "I wish the time had been longer!" I explained that we had just taken part in a kind of shortcut to contemplation, that centering prayer was only one way or aid into the contemplative process and that we would explore another way later in the evening.

Let's put contemplative prayer as a Christian's way of being in the world into perspective, I suggested. Too often, we are tyrannized by the recent past, the "We've *always* done it this way!" school of thought. "Always" can mean virtually anything from the last two years to the last two generations to the last couple of centuries. What happened before our limited "always"? I quoted from Thomas Keating: "A positive attitude toward contemplation characterized the first fifteen centuries of the Christian era. Unfortunately, a negative attitude has prevailed from the sixteenth century onward."[8]

I spent some time presenting an overview of those first fifteen hundred years of Christian spirituality when contemplation was considered to be the normal goal of everyone's (not just the mystics' or hermits') every prayer period, the historical clouding and fading of that understanding, and its resurrected life since Vatican II. Special attention was paid to the process of *lectio divina*, the circular prayer progression from *lectio* (scriptural reading or other spiritual intake to *meditatio* (discursive and imaginative consideration of the intake), to *oratio* (affective response) to *contemplatio* (active receptivity to the gift of God's presence). I suggested that the order of the four interdependent phases of *lectio divina* (literally divine reading) could fluctuate but that the inherent goal of this circular repetition was always the readiness for contemplation.

During the break, one couple was eager to express their amazement at the insight, new to them, that the subtle turnings of history and culture could so profoundly muddy the waters of our spiritual Tradition. Others nodded vigorously; one man bordered on outrage that in all his churchgoing years he had never been informed of this reality. Father remarked that the brief centering prayer, after some momentary anxiety, had relaxed and refreshed his body, mind, and spirit so thoroughly that he already was excited to try it again and perhaps go even deeper into a resting in God.

When all returned to their tables, obviously eager to proceed with an exercise in *lectio divina*, I read and then asked them each to read silently the story of Jesus' resurrection appearance to Mary Magdalene (John 20:11–18). I suggested that they read the passage three times, once for the story, once for the meaning, and a third time to imagine themselves as participants in the scene. They would have ten minutes for the reading and interior reflection. A bell tone would then sound and they would have ten more minutes as a period of response; for this purpose I had provided lemon yellow reflection booklets designed with a rainbow rush of glory and the scriptural word "He is not here; he is risen, just as he said" (Matt. 28:6). The focusing question I proposed was, "Where have *you* seen the risen Christ, lately?" After the final bell tone, fifteen minutes of sharing would follow.

The intensity of the small-group sharing was such that it was difficult to draw everyone back into the large group for closure. Individuals reported back in the closing session that they had known the risen Christ alive in their own lives through their participation in this prayer form. Others noticed a direct harmony between their response to this meditation and the quality of union with God they had felt during the centering prayer. I recommended books and articles to give more flesh to this introductory evening of contemplation. Above all, I invited them with vigor to continue the practice of contemplation. It is only ongoing and developing prayer, alone and with others, that draws us to *live* contemplatively rather than violently.

As I exchanged warm goodbyes with the O. L. parishioners, one older Polish woman commented, "I am so happy! You know, I prayed this way for years, but I never knew its name or that I could speak of it with others! The good God has shown me now!" Indeed, as these people went home into their own Galilees they were more certain that the risen Christ had preceded them there. I thought about the words of an old friend, St. Ignatius of Loyola, and breathed to myself, "Yup! There go twenty more 'contemplatives in action,' who will never again be satisfied with 'saying prayers!'" Spirituality is a way of living; contemplation is a way of being.

Three scenarios that served as modes of introduction to individual and corporate wholistic spirituality, three times three, times thirty, times three hundred. Yes, there were many more scenarios than these in our first year of PARISH ALIVE!, and there are as many scenarios as there are parishes in your own diocese, as many scenarios as your sacred imaginations can envision and create. Materials and resources abound. Which ones are right for your local situation? Your friends and neighbors, your parish, your church are often alone and hungry. Will you have the courage to replace maintenance attitudes with new ways of drawing them together? Will you feed them? Will you, parishioner or pastor, be daring enough to explore creative ways through the wilderness of your time and place so we all may stand as the Body of the risen Christ at this edge of an age?

· 4 ·

COME ASIDE AND
REST AWHILE

ITEM THREE of the PARISH ALIVE! brochure was so obvious and easy to formulate. What could be nicer for the folks in the city than to enjoy a pleasant Sunday afternoon ride down to the center by the sea for a two-hour session of prayer and reflection? What a helpful pause for busy lives! All five center team members were to be responsible for various of the seven monthly offerings between September and May; each presenter chose his or her favorite themes in spirituality. A participant could elect to come for one Sunday or the whole series.

The conference room was set up, the refreshments readied for the first of the "Come Aside" Sundays.

September 16th...No one came.

(Oh well, it's early in the program; the pastors just heard about PARISH ALIVE! last week.)

October 14th...No one came.

(Look at it this way: Everyone probably drove north today to see the changing leaves.)

December 2nd...No one came.

(We said to John, our chef, "Don't bother putting out refreshments next month until you see the whites of their eyes.")

He never even plugged in the coffee.

70

· 5 ·

COME ASIDE AND
REST AWHILE/TAKE TWO

A LITTLE DOSE of minor failure is always good for the soul!
It tends to put everything in perspective and causes ministerial
personnel to look heavenward and say, "You are God, and I am
not!" Our "Come Aside" miscalculation (read, "We batted zero,
folks!") reminded me of another humiliating incident twenty
years before. After completing a weekly seminar in Christian
Living with a group of thirty people for three months, I invited them for a come-back evening to discuss the fruits of their
learning experience. I remember walking into the seminar room
and exploding at the five smiling people who had accepted my
invitation. "Where *is* everybody? What's wrong with them?"
Smiles faded into looks of shocked rejection since those five
actually were the "everybody" for whom the evening was an
authentic need. It was nearly impossible to recoup the grace-
filled opportunity on that evening, but I did slowly internalize
an unforgettable two-part principle for ministry that has served
me well in the intervening years: (1) No matter how small the
group that arrives, even if it is just one person, Christ has come
to meet you; (2) if no one arrives, rethink; you have misjudged
the pastoral need.

Our situation led to the discovery that while the rationale for "Come Aside" was on target, the vehicle of Sunday
afternoons at the center was appealing to the presenters only.
Although we were correct in assuming that many parishioners

71

sought an opportunity to get some space from the ordinary patterned stress of everyday living in order to deepen the plane on which they live and be strengthened, the lure of our proximity to the seaside and quiet tree-lined paths was not relevant to family people on busy autumn Sundays.

Two solutions presented themselves: the first and obvious one was to shake off the dust and say, "Well, they don't know what they're missing!" and cross this item off next year's brochure. Defeatism and arrogance can be comfortable partners. The other possible response, of course, is second-order change; we could wait with fine-tuned listening, alert to the ways real people and real parishes desired to "Come Aside and Rest Awhile." In opting for the second choice, we allowed a foundational principle of PARISH ALIVE! to become enfleshed; the PARISH ALIVE! process refuses to predetermine pastoral needs. Rather, it grows organically from the really expressed needs of the people whom it serves.

During Christmas vacation, I was pleased to receive a phone call from a diocesan priest with whom I had once worked in religious education. He had just been appointed pastor of a semirural parish after the very long tenure of the previous pastor; he told me it was quite conservative and not at all used to change. Father envisioned a six-year plan for growth in spirituality within his new parish. He wondered if PARISH ALIVE! could offer him any ideas to launch his long-term plan. He had a strong desire to empower his people for peer ministry that would grow out of some sort of initial home-based parish retreat during which he might be better able to identify interested individuals. But we has to be careful, he said, not to frighten people off by anything that seemed too foreign to their previous church experience. He suggested that I might come to speak to the parish for four consecutive weeks in Lent on a weekday evening that was impossible for me. We considered every other day of the week, but four weeks in a row simply didn't work in my already packed schedule.

As we perused our respective calendars, I caught sight of the crossed out entry for a March Sunday afternoon, "Come Aside and Rest Awhile." Aha! Perhaps Father's parishioners at St. P's-in-the-Country needed to come aside, right where they were, from a time-honored treadmill church existence to a high-impact experience that might give them vital rest from the mundane and monotonous. Perhaps the form required here was the Lenten desert conversion opportunity of a wholistic parish mission. Perhaps they might "Come Aside and Rest Awhile," right in the familiar heart of their own parish church. "A mission," he spluttered. "I'll discuss this with some people but I don't think they'd ever go for that." Father made an appointment to come and talk it over at the center in early January.

When we met in my office, I proposed a four-evening mission (a term that everyone connects with their secure nostalgic Catholic past) with a difference. I said it was more possible for me to have different evening classes during one week covered by my partners on the team than four different editions of the same class covered over a month. Besides, the mission idea is dependent on total immersion in a compact time period; I pointed out that this process aimed at the persons most interested in spiritual life, and they would be willing to risk a week of their Lenten time on God's promise of fuller life. The mission itself would be equally based on the sevenfold sacramental life of the church and the emergence of a base community within the larger ecclesia. Nightly mission presentations would seek to combine wholistic spirituality with ritual and storytelling, thus to redefine in experiential terms the channels of grace available to us all, which have often grown wooden and stylized, taken-for-granted, unreflected habits of ordinary church life.

Father looked cautious but still interested, so I plunged ahead. The real difference here, I explained, is this important condition: you must assemble a parish mission team of approximately a dozen parishioners representing a cross section of your parish community who will meet weekly to share their

faith for a month in advance of the mission. On the Saturday
that precedes the mission itself, this team must commit itself
to a full day of reflection and preparation that I will facilitate.
You see, they will be directly involved in the ministry of the
mission. They will witness, administer nonsacramental anoint-
ing for healing, be available to pray with fellow parishioners,
prepare the sacred space each day, choose and lead music;
in other words, Father, you don't have to wait long for peer
ministry to evolve. Where there are willing people, there are
ministers of Christ's presence.

I took a deep breath. Not only at the mission itself, I continued, but in the weeks and months following, some members
of this team will offer six-week seminars to small groups of
parishioners who wish to continue growing together in the inward journey; this possibility will be explained to mission-goers,
and sign-up sheets for the seminars will be available every night
of the mission. There are numerous vehicles for these seminars
such as "Coming Alive in Faith," which has grown out of Isaiah 43 Ministries, and a longer course called "Pray" by Richard
Huelsman, SJ. These and many others have simple facilitator's
manuals that your parish mission team members can use with
a minimum of stress.

"Wait a minute," he said. "Number one: isn't this a little
ambitious? Number two: I've just arrived at the parish and I'm
hearing you say I must identify a dozen people capable of all
this and willing to do all this."

"Father," I replied, relegating objection number one to the
periphery, "all you need to do is find one individual willing to
chair this team and send that person down here to me."

"We'll see," he said, and left on that noncommittal note.

But Father remembered the young woman who had served
as a godmother to her nephew at last Sunday's baptism. During
the ceremony, he had invited those present to speak blessings
for the child, and the young woman had impressed him deeply
with the depth of her words, as well as the self-possession of
her manner and bearing. He saw a truly developed spiritual maturity in her person. So he went home to St. P's and asked if

she'd be interested in calling together a mission team. "Yes," M responded, without hesitation.

M was a bright young professional woman who had recently joined St. P's parish and who coincidentally had taken two courses at our center some years before. She had never been involved in church ministry but had a deep desire to have the church as home base in her life and to contribute her own talents so it might become more alive. When I met with her for an hour at the center, I introduced her to the booklet *Coming Alive in Faith*, and I asked her to attempt to gather a small group for whom she could facilitate a month-long faith-sharing experience, preparatory for the mission. M was willing, organized, and slightly terrified. She was new to the parish and did not yet know many people there. But she had a brother and sister-in-law there with whom to begin, and within a week there were nine others, men and women, old and young, married and single, who had agreed to give it a try. M wondered if anyone would speak during their first Monday evening meeting; she prepared an hour's worth of material, just in case a blank silence might cover the room. With delighted laughter, she informed me on the following Tuesday morning that she covered only a quarter of her notes because the other folks were so eager to enter into the sharing. Already, there were volunteers for premission publicity, mission liturgy planning, typing, and other practical tasks.

I set foot in St. P's for the first time over a month later, on a sparkling late winter Saturday morning, and found the dozen members of the "spirituality committee," as the premission team had named themselves, already a cohesive, sensitive, enthusiastic group. Here were people who were strangers to each other only five weeks before. That Saturday, in the rectory across from lake and woods, began with prayer and my explanation of the fundamental elements of a PARISH ALIVE! mission; it is an instrument for conversion to a deeper spiritual life dependent on collaborative ministry, productive of the formation of small basic prayer communities within the larger parish. The team understood that it would be the prototype of these basic communities, visible to the parishioners during the course of the mission; they already had such pride in their unified and purposeful identity that they had made and were wearing bright yellow badges featuring PARISH ALIVE! and their names connected by a rainbow, a symbol special to their parish. Rather than introducing themselves, they paired off and interviewed one another for ten minutes, returning to introduce their partner's identity, hopes, expectations, and reservations.

A practical overview of the four-day mission filled out the rest of the morning, and ministerial and logistic tasks were divided among the dozen team members. The hours after lunch were devoted to individual prayer and reflection time from which emerged each faith story. As each one told his or her story, patterns of grace, conversion, and hunger for life on a deeper plane emerged. It was from these stories that I chose four people to share their witness to God's faithful love in their lives on the various nights of the mission. The day ended with a ritual of reconciliation and harmony; the corporate spirit of the group was vitally alive with expectant faith.

That evening, I spoke at the parish Mass, inviting people to participate in the PARISH ALIVE! mission beginning on Monday evening. At the Masses on the following morning, M, chairperson of the mission team, echoed the same invitation. Each one-and-one-half-hour mission session that week would be based on one of the sacramental realities of the church — Initiation, Forgiveness, Healing, and Fulness of Eucharistic Community — and would include music, Scripture, prayer, a personal faith story from one of the team, my presentation, and a paraliturgical ritual in which all present would be invited to participate. On the final evening, the ritual would be a Mass, celebrated by the pastor. Crucial to the format of the mission evenings, an hour of hospitality in the church basement would follow each of our sessions in church. Holy hospitality is as important to PARISH ALIVE! as is depth experience in spirituality.

The mission was extremely successful. So many people opted to "Come Aside," even on the evening of the blizzard.

(People in the country tend to own four-wheel-drive vehicles.) Everyone present was deeply impressed by the sensible beauty of the symbolic decor appropriate to each evening, by the mission team, parishioners like themselves who had the courage to share their faith publicly, and by the sensitive power of the rituals. When the team members and I met for fifteen minutes before and after each evening session it was incredibly clear that their initial sense of purpose was flowering to a full-blown sense of empowerment. Surprised most profoundly night after night by what they saw and heard and did, they were in a brief time bonded by a grace both within and beyond themselves. One team member reported what a mission-goer had said to him over a cup of coffee and piece of "Hooray for St. P's PARISH ALIVE!" cake: "In the ten years I've been coming here to church nothing like this has ever happened! Finally, I believe that God's in church too!" Other team members jumped in with similar tales; all shook their heads in wonder.

During the mission's closing moments, Father was presented with a framed message done in calligraphy, welcoming him as new pastor, which one artistic woman had made. He was touched by that, and by the blessings these people of his prayed as they gathered around him; and I was delighted to accept the gift of a little glass bowl filled with rich soil. M explained to me and to the congregation that buried beneath the soil were a dozen morning glory seeds, representing each of the twelve members of the "spirituality committee." As the seeds came to flower in the spring, she and the other team members believed that they and the whole parish would continue to become more and more alive, springing from the foundation of their mission.

I didn't see the people of St. P's-in-the-Country again. They did not opt for any other of the formal PARISH ALIVE! offerings. They were ready to try their wings, "go their own route," the pastor had told me by phone. I was delighted by this message, since empowerment, the fruit of PARISH ALIVE!, demands the courage and conviction to hear the word and do it.

≈

Four months later, on a lazy July morning, I glanced out at my two window boxes filled with morning glories. Those dozen Lenten seeds had become a profusion of rich green leaves, healthy vines competing to win the climbing race up six fence posts of the deck, white and pink and lavender-blue trumpets singing to the rising sun. Those little flowers were not alone in their high summer flourishing.

M and I spoke on the phone midmorning of that day. She had news from St. P's-in-the-Country. The spirituality committee had indeed prepared and given their first six-week seminar directly following the PARISH ALIVE! mission; they had been instrumental in calling forth a parish planning day in the late spring for those who wished to work in a variety of ministries. The fifty people who had come together that day heard the spirituality committee proclaim the statement of purpose "that spirituality and prayer be the foundation and focus of all we do as a parish." This very evening there was to be an outdoor Mass under the large maple with the sunset scudding pink across their lake for their ministerial folks who were building community together in a parish becoming vibrantly alive. There were so many plans underway, so many additional people becoming involved in spirituality and small-group development, M and her friends had their hands full for the foreseeable future, and every endeavor was homegrown, tailor-made for their own parish up in the country!

A small voice inside me finally got around to addressing their pastor's initial winter question: Yes, Father, it *is* ambitious to enflesh the Gospel, with limited resources, right where you are. Jesus did it, though, with a small group of twelve. How about beginning in the middle, and giving it a try?

≈

During that Lenten season, another priest, the pastor from St. R's just outside the center city who had welcomed several other PARISH ALIVE! events to his church since September, also requested a wholistic parish mission. My colleague, Fr. Bob, presented the mission and welcomed over 150 parishioners on each of the four evenings as they elected to "Come Aside and Rest Awhile" in their own church hall. Shortly after the mission, St. R's pastor was interviewed for an article in our diocesan paper: "Ninety-five percent of the mission's very good turnout" availed themselves of an opportunity for reconciliation after the sessions, Father O. said. Father said he is impressed by PARISH ALIVE! because he sees in it a "real concern to meet the people of the parish at their level, in their needs, and in their place of worship." He also likes the endeavor's wholistic approach to spirituality. "The whole person goes to God in prayer," he says.[9] Father O. has since finished his term as pastor at St. R's and gone on to found a new parish, but his people continue in their efforts toward small faith group development and a living spirituality with a difference.

In the spring, an interparish group of twenty married couples requested a Sunday at the center, and Bob and I presented a day of spirituality entitled "Marriage as Ministry." St. T's-in-the-City negotiated a June Sunday, and sixty of their people came down to the center, to "Rest Awhile" and be refreshed.

These four examples provide some indication of the sense of mutuality that underlies the PARISH ALIVE! process. The process itself must continue to be willing to self-transform as it invites others to transformative spirituality. Too often, official renewal programs quickly rigidify materials and methodological components, providing an alternative status quo, still imposed from above or outside. PARISH ALIVE! assumes a natural internal development, based on expressed pastoral need. The variance among the four Gospels seems to be the best evidence for this assumption: four proclamations of the same Good News, four uniquely different styles and structures, based on the pastoral needs of the four very different communities of Matthew, Mark, Luke, and John.

When the PARISH ALIVE! brochure was reprinted for the second year, "Come Aside and Rest Awhile" was still the third item; but it had grown up and filled out, just as any other perennial the gardener plants. Now there were two possibilities for those seeking deeper growth in spirituality: Come Aside in your parish for a wholistic parish mission, Come Aside at the center as a parish group for a Sunday afternoon of spirituality, including a light supper. (Jesus always said, "Give these people something to eat.") Both possibilities are arranged on request.

PARISH ALIVE! is just like life. You learn and grow through the learning and growing.

· 6 ·

ONE IN MIND AND HEART

THREE TIMES in Mark's chapters 8, 9, and 10, the Ben-Zebedee brothers and the rest of that motley dozen of hand-picked leaders, are found fumbling around looking for seats of wisdom, power, and honor. As they berate Jesus, one another, and everybody else in the vicinity, one can imagine that Jesus just might have thrown his hands up in the air, "Abba, is *this* really it? After all, if you happen to be the Savior of the world, founder of a church, you've got to have a dependable and unified middle-management team, don't you?" "Son, keep working at it; do the best with what you've got!" The Gospels record that Jesus indeed continued to "work at it," continued the patient, endless dialogue with his chosen twelve, who in the end scattered and ran for the hills. However, after the end, eleven returned strengthened in the Spirit of unity, courage, and love and spent their lives as servant-witnesses "to the ends of the earth" (Acts 1:8).

And indeed, the Spirit of Jesus has gone on "working at it" through all the generations of the church. God knows, human beings in ecclesial and parish leadership today are just as plagued by the petty pitfalls of human nature as their prototypical predecessors in Galilee.

If you are a working member of the parish term, reflect for a moment on the relative percentages of time spent in this last calendar year arguing with a colleague in the rectory about who gets to book the church hall on a particular date as opposed to the hours you've spent with team members in prayer, reflection, and spiritual growth. Unfortunately, there's not much time for the latter, you muse. On the other hand, the pitched battle to determine the king (queen) of the hall *did* take an hour to wage, even though the outcome was predetermined. You, with your one hundred confirmation candidates and sponsors, would get the sacristy because he, with his seven baptismal preparation couples, always used the hall. "After all," he had said, attempting benevolence, "that's why we had the parish hall air-conditioned! I mean, some of those seven expectant mothers might be uncomfortable in the small, airless sacristy."

This and other "pastoral planning meetings" of similar import are the clear result of competition replacing compassion. Where this replacement is carried to extremes, the choice to live and minister creatively finally yields to its diametric opposite, the choice, often by default, to live and minister violently. The tendency to violence (and I include in that term irreverence for one another as persons, as well as every kind of power game) that can infect the ministers of God's word and work is so often bred from exhaustion, workaholism, burnout. Most often no one is ministering to the ministers. Furthermore, the ministers are unaware that they have the same needs for growth in community and spirituality as their people.

I recall a woman, an experienced DRE, who returned to her home state seeking a position in her field. During her interview at a parish, she asked the pastor with what regularity the team of priests, deacon, professional religious educators, school principal, music director, and parish secretary prayed together, and with what frequency these people met for days of reflection or spiritual enrichment. He drew a blank but did mention that his DRE's salary was higher than anyone else's in the diocese. She refused the position when it was offered to her.

One of the aims of PARISH ALIVE! is to raise the consciousness of parish clergy and other ministry professionals beyond a theology of exemption. If the parishioners need further teaching, so do they; if the parishioners need a growing delight and proficiency in prayer, so do they; if the parishioners need to become vulnerable enough to share their faith, so do they. As

Father Gerard Broccolo of the archdiocese of Chicago stated at a recent conference in Washington, D.C., "All ministry is a *limited* share in the priestly ministry of Jesus Christ."[10] When any of us de-emphasize and finally discard the all important qualifier "limited," we have removed ourselves from ministry and entered the world of ecclesial or parochial bureaucracy. On the other hand, when we face our human poverty and taste our human hunger, we become liberated; our laughter at our own littleness frees us to seek together the sustenance we need.

"One in Mind and Heart" is the facet of PARISH ALIVE! that seeks to address this liberation with professional parish persons. When we first described this item as "days of reflection, or consultation, for pastors and parish teams...in the parish or at the center," we did not yet have in mind the multiplicity of forms this might take. In fact, the variety of requests that emerged simply indicates again that unity has absolutely nothing to do with uniformity when we speak of personal human transformation through spirituality.

The first request for consultation was an invitation to a deanery meeting in early September to discuss with pastors from a specific area of the diocese the possibilities PARISH ALIVE! might hold for them. It was a formidable experience to hear this captive ordained audience stumble through opening prayer, to watch half of them nod off to sleep as the speaker who preceded me addressed them and to know that I had little chance of waking them, to stand to speak and be caught in a time warp that convinced me I was back once again addressing resentful confirmation parents forced into my presence by the threat of an *"absolutely* required meeting." The wonderfully enthusiastic and supportive pastor-dean who had invited me told me at the conclusion of the meeting that he was very pleased; this had certainly been a successful session! I must have appeared dumbfounded because he added, "You should see most of our other meetings!"

I was more alarmed than surprised when he called me

within a few days to ask if I'd be willing to present an "Advent Afternoon" of experiential spirituality for the priests of this deanery and their parish staffs in early December. "You're really willing to take that risk?" I asked incredulously. "I am," he answered. "Oh, well, it's always a pleasure to collaborate with other fools for Christ. I'll be there."

The difference in that same room in December was the absence of institutional peer pressure. Only those arrived who really desired to pray together, together with their DREs and pastoral ministers (women!). I had prepared a variation on the evening at St. P's Episcopal, with more faith sharing and visioning time built in, and a bit more emphasis on the Advent kerygma. I watched these pastoral people both laugh and cry together as they prayed away the brief December afternoon.

Lesson: oneness in mind and heart can never be legislated; it depends solely on the delicate and reverent relationship of invitation and free response.

Several and sundry consultative meetings went on through the first autumn:

— A deacon from a parish near the center made an appointment to discuss first steps and basic materials that he might use to introduce spirituality to the volunteer ministry groups in his parish; up to this point the groups' thrust had been doing rather than being. We made plans to continue our conversations.

— St. T's staff and council of ministries listened eagerly to PARISH ALIVE! proposals for growth in the spirituality of leadership through the media of a coming weekend retreat at the center and Track 1 of "Greater Things Than I...," which they agreed should be offered to their spirituality committee in the early spring.

— Individual pastors requested one-to-one meetings at the center and in their parishes to discuss their distinctive local needs and to begin to set up possible processes to initiate.

— I was invited to speak at the annual Parish Alliance

meeting where pastoral teams and small-group leaders gathered to share the progress and concerns of those parishes restructuring into small groups.

These and many other instances of PARISH ALIVE!'s "One in Mind and Heart" developed an early awareness of the collaboration that was possible between professional parish ministers and the spirituality resources of the center; they amplified and fine-tuned a readiness for parish staff events like those that follow.

On the third of eight weekly evenings that one parish staff requested to put themselves in touch as a body with the spirituality of faith group development, I felt a slight "disturbance in the field." These eight courteous individuals were beginning to exhibit symptoms of discomfort as they heard snatches of disparity in one another's descriptions of the "unified vision" of their roles in the projected means of spiritual growth for their parish. People shifted in their chairs; smiles became semipleasant stony expressions that further devolved into jawjutting silences.

"Forgive me, if I'm mistaken," I interjected, "but I sense another agenda someplace just beneath the surface." With that permission granted, the manneristic minuet of polite Christian colleagues broke into a minor brawl. "He said...!" "She said...!" "They promised...!" All the "interventions" were accusations and therefore, as at Babel, no one could hear or understand the others.

Incarnational spirituality demands praxis, not theory; that is, we deal with the really real, not the disembodied ideal. If we are in search of greater unity of mind and heart, let's make an effort to discover what it is that unites us in this present moment and what it is that possibly divides us. So, I said, if you will permit me to deviate from the agenda we all expected to follow this evening, I suggest that you allow me to facilitate an I-statement needs assessment among you. "Well, okay, but *we* all agree that *she* was wrong."

Either "I" or no one at all! I insisted. The single ground
rule for this assessment is that anyone is free to make any
statement as long as it begins with "I need" or "I feel." No one
may challenge or refute these "I" statements; we will simply
receive them and list them on the board.

Think about God's conversation with Moses in Exodus 3.
Moses was in trouble and confused; so were the people he represented, held in Egyptian bondage as they were, the elders
of Israel embattled by their fears, anxieties, and recrimina-
tions. God refrained from remarks like "*You* people better get
your act together!" or "*They* are certainly a sniveling bunch of
wimps!" God simply said "I AM" (Exod. 3:16). When Moses
reported this divine self-identification back to the elders, all
of them knew where God stood and, by relational association,
that they themselves stood protected by Divine Presence and
therefore capable of action. They were freed from the immobi-
lization engendered by blame-saying, and soon thereafter they
freed themselves from the external slavery of Egypt.

Any group whose function includes leadership, visioning,
and decision making is crippled by the avoidance of "I" statements; dysfunction escalates immeasurably when that group
is "religious." If we are "religious," "we," "you," and "they"
statements assume the added weight of moral judgments and
insinuate the speaker's own impeccability. Resentment engendered by group members' self-righteous indignation and the
tacit accompanying claim of personal "holiness," have held captive parish teams, religious communities, and diocesan councils
for years of nonproductivity. This stagnation finally results in
morbidity as vital members cross their individual discourage-
ment thresholds and leave. If we take the "religious" group to
a deeper plane and it claims spirituality as its source, sustenance, and goal, then the refusal to communicate by means
of "I" statements becomes a scandalous contradiction in terms.
My point of reference has ceased to be my true Self, the place
within me where God dwells. I escape into the anonymous
finger-pointing realm of the corporate "we" and "they" debate.

This parish staff of eight agreed to the assessment and came up with twenty-four individual "I" statements in answer to my question, "What do you absolutely need to be a member of this group?" Some statements were philosophical and foundational, like "I need to *understand* whether this group is primarily for mutual spiritual support or primarily for task accomplishment, or both." Other statements were practical, like "I need a telephone chain to be established among us so I am not handicapped by surprise changes in schedules and plans." When all eight persons were satisfied that the list on the board was a fair representation of what they wanted to say, I asked them to reread the statements carefully to see if there were any that were completely unacceptable to any individual. "No," they decided (although it is perfectly appropriate at this point in the process to state that you *cannot* live with an expressed need of another member). Well, then, does anyone need further clarification from the author of any of the statements? A few requests answered by refinements or amplifications followed.

Every one of these essential needs must be addressed by the group! An inclusive community of eight or an inclusive parish-community of eight hundred requires that every "I" be reverenced. Whether his or her greatest need is also mine is not the issue here. What *is* at issue is (a) my willingness to accept my own vulnerability and responsibility for standing forth in my own truth and (b) to accord the same essential human dignity to the others. This it not to say that every accepted need and desire of every member will be perfectly and speedily fulfilled by the group; it *is* to say that now we know where we stand and we can proceed to address what is really real for us. The stumbling blocks of hidden agendas, silent judgments, and denials of personal responsibility have been cleared from our path into the future.

These staff members marvelled at meeting's end at the sense of ease and peace they felt now that they had agreed to disagree. They laughed as they realized how tightly their very fear of conflict had bound them to a veiled hostility and incapacity for meaningful progress. It was heartening for me to hear them prioritize foundational and practical needs and schedule open discussion of these for their next several weekly meetings. I projected into the future as I imagined the exponential growth in unity this staff could experience and how they as a small group of faith-sharing Christians would not only plan, but become the microcosmic paradigm for the restructuring of their entire parish.

Another parish staff interested in "One in Mind and Heart" requested a facilitated day of reflection and prayer for a date in late January. "We'd like something sort of upbeat and spiritual," their representative suggested, "something like 'Appreciating the Love of God through Our Differing Gifts.'" The proposed title was a bit generic and didn't give me much to go on so I called back. "What's the general mood of the staff these days?" I asked. "Oh, terribly depressed!" she replied. "I mean the war in the desert, the closed banks; everything seems up for grabs, nothing to hold on to. That's why Father's been keeping the homilies cheerful; no sense confusing the parish more than they already are. After all, they get enough of *that* on TV! We all do! You know, that's why the staff really needs the Day of Reflection, to escape for a few hours, put things on the bright side for a change!" Mmm-hmmm.

The goal of spiritual direction is to look squarely at "what's happening" and follow its lights and shadows, down deep to "what's really going on." A happy, "superspiritual" escape hatch, masquerading as a day of prayer, seemed inauthentic to me so I decided to go with "terrible, depressed, confused." I went a step further to "terrified, disoriented, hopeless" as I prepared the day of reflection. To reflect on anything other than "what is" is sheer fantasy and a waste of everyone's energy. God simply does not live in "what is not."

As the session began, early morning sun streamed through a high window, highlighting the earth icon that was background for a bowl of baptismal water and the nearly burned down paschal candle from last year's Easter; I played an instrumental tape, "Peace in the Puzzle." Today we would immerse ourselves in the interrelatedness of Peace, Power, and Vulnerability. I introduced the theme with two anecdotes, dealing with the current and desperate confusion that lack of peace was causing. The first was a homey story of my fourteen-year-old daughter, who sat last week watching the coming of the war on TV. Two juxtaposed flickering images caused her to stiffen and gasp. The president of our nation was shown praying in church for speedy victory; the president of our "enemy" nation was shown kneeling on his prayer rug, presumably with an identical prayer on his lips. The child was angry, "Who is *he* praying to?" she exploded. The second was a recent article from a local paper, "Whose Side Is God On?" The black writer quotes his "theological Harlem friend, Booker Leroi Johnson": "My grandmother say you never forget any of us. She be always singin' that song, 'His eye is on the sparrow, and I know he watches me....' And that be my point, Lord: who you be watchin' over in this war?" Booker goes on remonstrating with God and finally sighs and concludes, "The real test of peace be at home as much as it be in the Middle East."[11] Both stories connected us simply and squarely to our own current experience of shared human powerlessness. To be able to survive and grow emotionally and spiritually, we must stand openly in the heart of our human condition, this condition of vulnerability, and get in touch with our immutably rooted personal identity.

And *now*, let us pray. We entered prayer by listening to a native American chant, "We all come from God, and unto God we shall return; like a stream flowing back to the ocean, like a ray of light returning to the sun."[12] As we listened over and over to the basic human rhythm, we became still and centered. Before I began the guided meditation, I suggested that a point would be reached in the inner journey that they would wish to make indelible in their memories. It would be an experience of profound peace and meaningful purpose that they might find helpful to re-experience during anxious moments in times beyond this particular day. When that moment in the prayer comes, I offered, let your body help your mind and spirit to imprint the experience for future access. Just make a simple physical gesture; for instance, place your hands in your lap, palms together in the traditional prayer posture, or any other simple gesture comfortable for you. Later on, when you wish to re-experience that inner peace, make the gesture with your hands, and your body will help your spirit to remember. The conjoined participation of body, mind, and spirit is basic for wholistic prayer. So too, memory, imagination, and will as functions of the praying intellect are as traditional as St. Ignatius, who cited their essential engagement, and as contemporary as the field of sacred psychology explored in our own day by pioneers like Jean Houston.

I changed the tape to "Wave Tones" for the creative visualization prayer and led the staff members on a twenty-minute descent through time and space to the moment of their birth, and up through their childhoods and growing years to the moment when they first "left home," either literally or figuratively. As they imagined their youthful selves, setting off for the future, both fear and exultation appeared on their closed-eyed countenances. As they each freeze-framed that inner instant, I asked them to listen carefully to the Voice that they may not have recognized at the time, but that they hear now, "You are my son, my daughter, my beloved; my favor rests on you." As they listened the second time, absorbing the assurance of their true and wonderful identity, I suggested the simple physical gesture I had mentioned earlier. Gently, I led them back to the present moment, where they each found a blank reflection booklet; they would have fifteen minutes to journal their prayer experience by answering the question "What was it like for you when you first experienced your own first 'leaving home,' your own call to identity?" This reflection was in the context of the threefold fundamental human question as framed by the artist Paul Gauguin, "Who am I? Where did I come from? Where am I going?" I mentioned that now, and as long as they wished for the time to come, they could re-experience the inner power of the divine answer they had heard within by repeating the palms-together gesture and allowing this physical reminder to be a way to touch into the spiritual reality. The one-to-one sharing that followed the reflection gave each person the opportunity to claim their God-given identity, permeated both by vulnerability and empowerment.

During my presentation on the baptism of Jesus, including his temptation in the wilderness and his empowered emergence into the Galilean ministry (Mark 1:9–15), we looked to the water of our own baptism and its paschal cycle of renewal. We saw that we have not only the gift of personal identity but a share in the Christic identity. Through our own baptisms, we have plunged with Jesus into the Jordan to emerge validated, incorporated, and commissioned. We claimed our share in that royal, priestly, and prophetic identity as we closed the morning with the Taizé mantra "Laudate Dominum" and a ribbon of memory ritual that connected us with both spiritual ancestors and descendants.

After lunch we reassembled and sang "Center of My Life" by Paul Inwood and prepared to look at vulnerability/powerlessness as perhaps our most sublime gift. I quoted Martin Buber:

> Doom becomes more oppressive in every new eon, and the return more explosive. And the theophany comes ever closer....History is a mysterious approach to closeness. Every spiral of its path leads us into deeper corruption and at the same time into more fundamental return. But the God-side of the event whose world-side is called return is called redemption.[13]

Together we prepared to view a sixty-minute video, part 5 of the twelve-cassette *Canticle to the Cosmos* by Brian Swimme, based on Thomas Berry's twelve principles of a functional cosmology. "A functional cosmology is an account of where we are, where we come from, what we are doing, and where we are going. It is the story of our time."[14] Berry, a Passionist priest who calls himself a "geologian" (theologian of the earth), insists that we as Christians need to know the "new story," that is, newly accessible in our times, for the first time, that he expresses in his first principle for understanding the universe and the role of the human in the universe process. "The universe, the solar system, and the planet earth in themselves and in their evolutionary emergence constitute for the human community the primary revelation of that ultimate mystery whence all things emerge into being."[15] Part 5 of the *Canticle* is entitled "Destruction and Loss" and coincides with Berry's Principle Five: "The universe has a violent as well as harmonious aspect, but it is consistently creative in the larger arc of its development."[16]

To come in touch with the macrocosmic dimension of the paschal mystery is to raise your sights from the terrifying constriction of your own painful personal fears. The film that this staff viewed on their day of reflection obviated the delusion that the elimination of resistance, trial, and loss is good. They began to picture themselves as individuals and as a group, involved in the much wider story of the sanctification of the whole human race, whole planet earth, whole of creation, a story that necessitates cycles of life, death, and resurrection. They came to understand that the discerning question is not "How can we keep everybody's mind off the current pain and go on with business as usual?" but rather, "In the midst of all that is really and terribly real, how can we live a noble life by creating a feast?" They heard the hopeful truth that all human creativity comes out of working against obstacles, that the terror of loss offers the best opportunity to unite with what is real.

Reflection on the video began with a journaling exercise in pamphlets imprinted with a crown-of-thorns-ringed earth and the question, "In the midst of this particular winter of destruction, what is the choice for creativity that I make?" Sharing personal choices led to developing corporate choices for themselves as a ministering staff. These were people with a restored sense of self and a revitalized sense of mission. We closed with a prayer bidding hello to the New Year with all its uncertainties and opportunities and by singing the "Prayer for Peace" by David Haas. These were people no longer so afraid of fear; this was a parish staff who had opened their minds and hearts to a new look at truth and received unity and peace as gifts of their shared humanity.

As months went by, I heard more and more stories of the

new life and vitality that marked that parish. The staff's courageously human stance was bearing fruit for the parish, even in a season of blight.

PARISH ALIVE! believes that human is holy.

· 7 ·

SEASON OF REFRESHMENT

IT WAS A RAW FRIDAY NIGHT during the time of year that academia calls interterm, the season the church refers to as ordinary time, the slushy month the folks have nicknamed the post-Christmas "blahs." Could there be a better moment to begin our first PARISH ALIVE! weekend retreat at the center? Three dozen people from three different parishes sat in a circle in the conference room, their attention drawn to the circle's center.

A purple-and-blue woven cloth was flung on the floor; upon it spread the present season in miniature. A huge angular piece of driftwood, empty arms branching in all directions, was dominant. Each crevice and crooked wooden cranny half-hid another shrivelled, empty surprise; a pile of brown and withered leaves, an abandoned swallow's nest, seashells whose occupants had long fled. At the near corner of the gnarled and lonely forest was a simple girl of carved brown wood, sitting back on her heels, her hands open at her sides, her wooden eyes longing toward the distance. What she saw spinning from the highest, farthest branch, through the tangle of the woods, was a mysterious promise. A large and delicate crystalline bauble hung there, backlighted by tiny blue glass lamps, like a tear drop catching rainbows, a star in a bare winter tree. Gentle and deft, the first alluring notes of George Winston's "Winter into Spring" played in the background.

≈

For our "Seasons of Refreshment" program we decided from the outset to leave the beaten path of typically liturgical-cycle-type seasonal retreats. When Advent or Lenten weekends are announced to the parish, they usually carry the pious baggage of "sacrificial obligation." Often, no one notices that the juxtaposition of these two words ranges from mutually exclusive to downright contradictory. Sacrifice carries the notion of gift made holy and *freely* given. In addition to the grammatical gaff, the penitential nature of Lent and the prophetic waiting of Advent tend to become intermingled and confused. The rich rhetoric and rubrics of these most popular of church seasons can devolve into habitual obscurity, their efficacy as flowing fountains of spiritual awareness weakened by religious overkill.

An alternative is to seek the sacred in the primal earthy seasons, which are themselves the ancient and natural basis for liturgical cycles. Rabbi Abraham Heschel has reminded us that "Just to be is a blessing...just to live is holy." One object of PARISH ALIVE! is to redeem this universally, if tacitly, held human affirmation of creation from the confinement of institutional vocabulary and forms. Designing seasonal retreats that deliberately evoke and use primal human responses to the fearsome fading of light and warmth during the days we now call Advent, or the sensed promise of the reemergence of spring from the hard winter earth during the days we now call Lent, further develops the Christian as prophet. "The task of prophetic ministry...is to nurture, nourish and evoke a consciousness and perception alternative to the consciousness and perception of the dominant culture around us."[17] This "dominant culture" includes the prevailing religious culture that names and narrows "the holy" to something that happens only in church.

≈

As we return to the retreat's opening session, we see that each participant holds a cherry pink weekend schedule, designed with a graphic of a leafless winter tree and the title "In the Depth of the Winter...I finally learned that within me, there lay an invincible summer" (Albert Camus). The schedule itself reveals that the weekend will include three one-hour presentations, much time for personal meditation, liturgical Evening and Morning Prayer, Eucharist, small-group reflection and sharing, and a contemporary video, "The Global Brain."

The inner logic of the retreat employs both traditional forms and visionary concepts to create an experience for the retreatants wherein they may know and name their own spirituality. The interplay of spiritual treasures old and new will offer the closely woven opportunity of at-homeness/adventure. Thomas Merton's friend, Brother David Steindl-Rast, speaks of the courage of the pilgrim within us that overcomes the polarization of the settler and the wanderer who also live within: "The compulsive settler within us dares to be committed, but fears being on the road. The aimless wanderer within us dares to be on the road, but fears being committed."[18] During this weekend, we are pilgrims together who conjoin these two darings in the heart of hope. Steindl-Rast concludes, "Hope is the openness for surprise. Hope is the virtue of the pilgrim."

I based the presentation themes on the second chapter of Fran Ferder's *Words Made Flesh: Scripture, Psychology and Human Communication*. Ferder's ideas on "Listening as a Biblical Stance toward Creation" include three phases of listening.[19] These phases — Attending, Following, and Responding — became the topics for my Friday evening, Saturday, and Sunday morning talks. Attending, of course, simply means paying close attention. It is an attitude of prayer that requires silent focusing on what I see and hear outside myself, as well as in the inscape of my heart and spirit. In the end of wintertime landscape, paying close attention reveals deadness, now wearily waiting for shoots of new life. In the mirror-image that is my inner life I might take a quiet inventory to see where there are hollow losses and empty spaces.

Each person received an inventory sheet to assist this interior journey. The sheet featured a quotation from Nikos Kazantzakis, "What we call non-existent is what we do not desire enough," and a dozen questions reflecting possible personal losses, from the loss of life's purpose to the loss of the gift of laughter. In the corner of the paper, as would be true of various sheets to be distributed this weekend, was a line drawing of snowy woods, a single set of footprints marking an invisible path. In this evening's personal prayer, to identify and embrace the specific empty place in my own life would be the beginning of expectation of new life. As the participants went off to pray, they also received a list of Scripture texts promising God's fulness, for example, a word from Lamentations (3:19–24), "The favors of Yahweh are not all past... every morning they are renewed." A thought from St. John of the Cross set a framework for these passages, "If you wish to be sure of the road you tread on, you must close your eyes and walk in the dark."

On Saturday morning we considered the component of listening that we name Following as "staying with another." Jesus provides the example as he goes off into the hills alone to stay with Abba. And when others want to continue listening to him, they ask where he lives. "Come and see," he responds, and some do. Can we pilgrim in that pattern today?

The guided meditation, down into our own always available inner place apart, was the first experiencing of centering for some who were present. One young woman was initially shocked to discover that at the deepest moment of the centering experience, she found herself held in the living memory of a time when she was scuba diving in the Caribbean. Just as it had happened then, she found herself today floating in a vital, nonresistant sea of peace, laced with light, and herself perfectly aware of a joyous strength in her own person. She was deeply moved when I suggested that this memory had opened her to "religious experience," as she had never been told nor had she imagined that "prayer" could *feel* like the fullness of life.

There was time then for everyone to Follow, to go off, perhaps down to the sea alone, or into the woods and meadows, to pay attention to the Creator thinly veiled by creation. Perhaps, during their active reflection, someone might come upon the open barn. He or she would first notice the external signs of winter there: the abandoned nests of barn swallows long

ago flown south, the drifted snow piled in doorways, the wind
whistling through turn-of-the-century shingles. This noticing is
not yet prayer. Soon the visual realities will fade and blur as
the pilgrim stands there, growing quieter, seeking for meaning
in the heart of this chill and desolate place. Still, this is not
prayer. But then the winter barn itself begins to whisper secrets
to the pilgrim, telling tales of its own barrenness and the pilgrim's. Finally they become one, winter and the pilgrim, and
together they sing a silent song of the longing for the return of
summer life. And the lyrics begin to speak of their joy, as they
anticipate the time of flowering that is promised by the very
fact of the present diminishment and death. This is prayer.

Another pilgrim will walk by the deserted shore line; yet another will stand beneath a naked shivering birch tree. Each one
has followed Jesus to a lonely place and with him has found
the plenitude of grace.

Each retreatant had received a reflection booklet with the
winter woods picture and St. Paul's words, "May the Lord direct your hearts into God's love and Christ's perseverance"
(2 Thess. 3:5). They were asked to journal their solitary meditation experience and to share these thoughts in small groups
with the other members of their own parish. Each period
of small-group sharing over the weekend alternated between
single-parish and mixed-parish groupings.

(Do you remember the six women from St. T's-in-the-City,
newly named as the parish spirituality committee? These six
were now sitting in the conference room, sharing their sacred
afternoon experiences. By Sunday morning, the level of their
bonding would initiate a decision among them to talk about
meeting at one another's homes for shared prayer! "We need
this!" "Yes, *especially* if we're going to serve *other people!*"
Furthermore, before leaving the center after Sunday brunch,
they would *all* sign up for "Greater Things ... " and two of them
would make appointments to begin monthly spiritual direction
sessions!)

During the interparish sharing groups, retreatants whose
communities were considered quite dissimilar found both com-

mon ground and novel directions. At the dinner table, faith sharing spilled over into practical considerations for building parish community according to varying styles and differing emphases in spirituality.

Two retreat highlights, their roots separated by centuries, were especially challenging to the participants because both facets were new to all of them. The first was the celebration of liturgical prayer other than Eucharistic liturgy. Many saw the possibility of introducing the idea of occasional or regular/ seasonal solemn Morning or Evening Prayer in their parishes, a traditional feature of the official worship of the church that they had thought was reserved only to monasteries and convents. The second, a thirty-minute video, "The Global Brain" by Peter Russell, provided an invitation to consider the wholistic nature of an evolving human spiritual consciousness. The film's narrative closes with these words from playwright Christopher Fry:

> The human heart can go to the lengths of God
> Dark and cold we may be, but this
> is no winter now. The frozen misery
> of centuries breaks, cracks, begins to move.
> The thunder is the thunder of the floes,
> the thaw, the flood, the upstart spring.
> Thank God our time is now when wrong
> comes up to face us everywhere,
> Never to leave us till we take
> The longest stride of soul folk ever took.
> —Affairs are now soul size.
> > The enterprise
> > is exploration unto God.
> What are you waiting for?
> It takes so many thousand years to wake,
> But will you wake for pity's sake?[20]

To live the spiritual transition from winter into spring, as that movement began to appear to the retreatants, was to live in mysterious cyclical oneness with the Lord of the Paschal

Mystery, with oneself, with nature, with the whole earth itself, as well as with Tradition.

The third function of listening is Responding, and on Sunday mid-morning we explored that reality. In the context of prayer, is Responding a verbal answer, or is it an action, a doing? Can mere words be the appropriate response to the Good News of God's faithful death-to-resurrection love in our lives? We looked together at the white bowl of fuchsia tulips that now exploded with out-of-season color in the miniature winter scene that had remained central throughout the weekend. Now the little wooden girl at prayer was surrounded by small twinkling candle lights. A path of lights stretched out into her once lonely empty woods and ended at the bowl of blooming springtime, their light dancing through the still suspended bauble. Together we sang a mantra of glad surprise, its words from Psalm 8:

> Who are we, O Lord, that you should care for us?
> Your heavens are high, our dwelling place is low.[21]

Over and over we sang in harmony and entered into the action of a ritual of reverencing; one person stood and invited each other person, one by one, to approach. As the song continued, that person bowed silently to each one who approached and gently placed his or her hand on the other's face or took the hand of the other and looked quietly and deeply into the other's eyes. No words were spoken; there was simply a profound appreciation of the other person for the gift he or she is, one with whom God is pleased to dwell. Just as at the eucharistic celebration the evening before, Christ was alive and palpably present as this ritual of reverencing continued the sharing of the Body of Christ among these men and women as the retreat closed.

≈

What effects did this brief "Season of Refreshment" have back in the parishes to which the retreatants returned? Each of the participants returned to their home parishes and their volunteer ministries in the midst of a dreary January day, bearing gifts of springtime and seeds of new life. They went home running, as eager as the two Emmaus youths ran the seven miles back to Jerusalem, to share with the others what they had seen and heard, to experience with the others the Lord who had risen from death to life. Hadn't their hearts burned within them as he spoke to them on the way, in the very depth of winter?

Be prepared for a surprise as we follow some of these refreshed pilgrims and their friends back to "Emmaus" five months in the future!

· 8 ·

GREATER THINGS THAN I
SHALL YOU DO . . .

JESUS threw a pebble in the pond. And a very small and obscure pond it was. Only twelve concentric ripples radiated outward from the humbly splashed center. But the pond fed the stream, and the stream fed the river, and the river fed the sea, guaranteeing eternal return. Jesus of Nazareth, the apprentice carpenter turned cosmologist, evidently believed that "less is more" and that no energy expended is ever lost or destroyed but simply expands in ever-widening circles, "always, even until the end of the world" (Matt. 28:20). He had designs on the human race that he entrusted to the littlest and the least. Do we still appreciate the master plan or does stone skimming on the little parish pond appear too simplistic in the sophisticated complexity of our ecclesial worldview?

After all, Jesus' Ministry Training Program for the twelve was quite casual and homey; manuals and codes of criteria were unheard of in his neighborhood. None of the twelve had degrees, of course, so there was no sense in Jesus offering advanced courses. He simply found people where they were and talked to them in the language of their common humanity. His own stance toward them and toward the ultimate reality of Abba seemed so naturally interconnected, harmonious, and attractive; what was there to do but follow him home? Perhaps he would disclose his secret. Jesus' words and works were undeniably dynamic and he insisted that he was inviting all people to share in them, but how, they wondered. One disciple finally framed the core question, "What must we do if we are to do the works that God wants?" Jesus responded, "This is working for God: you must have faith in the one he has sent" (John 6:28–29). So it was the essential "work of believing" that seemed to underlie both discipleship and ministry. Aha! If believing is work, and in fact the preeminent work, there must be room for development and expansion in the faith I already "have." Faith must be something more and something else than the static spiritual commodity I thought I possessed.

"Sharing the Light of Faith," issued by the United States Catholic Conference in March 1979, suggested that the *goal* of all catechesis is "maturity of faith." Faith-sharing groups and their leaders in our parishes have often been unable to make the extrapolation, that "maturity" includes the notion that where must be stages of faith that are more and less mature, that faith is a developmental reality on both an individual and a corporate basis. Furthermore, faith-language is heard and interpreted in as many vernaculars as there are individual levels of faith existing in a particular gathered group. The perfectly clear approach to the mystery of God-with-us taken by an individual small-group leader may mean something uniquely different to each of the ten members seated around her. She has opened herself to frustration and fruitlessness if she fails to understand this clearly. Little by little, she begins to feel incompetent as group members either drift away or make little visible progress in their faith-sharing and community-building activities. She feels her limitations keenly and finally says "Father, I think you'd better find someone else for this ministry," or, loath to relinquish her title of "leader," she blames the group for their lack of "commitment." She continues to attend quarterly leaders' meetings where she is lulled and soothed by listening to woes and complaints similar to her own. "We know this small-group thing is supposed to work!" comments a leader from a neighboring parish. "After all, we all attended the big conference two years ago and listened to that speaker from [another section of the country]. Gee, we've been using her materials ever since! How come it's not working here?"

Our cultural fixation with the better mousetrap or the "perfect" methodology is often a blind for the denial of our own personal limitations or a diversion from the acknowledgment of our personal responsibility to grow in creative competence.

"Greater Things Than I..." as a vital facet of PARISH ALIVE! is based on the belief that small-group or base community leaders must be empowered in spirituality and style of leadership that includes a growing spiritual, functional, and relational proficiency. This growth in personal competence demands a departure from the typical church leadership stance of one who "does" toward an embrace of myself as one who "is." I become the stone that Jesus chooses to throw into the still water, and I empower the water to thrill and move, stirring greater waters far beyond itself.

"Greater Things..." proposes three multi-week tracks to serve the competence development needs of small-group leaders: Track 1 includes "Understanding Individual and Corporate Faith Development" and the "Art of Dialogue"; Track 2 highlights "Facilitation of Faith Development Groups"; Track 3 offers "Skills in Spiritual Companioning." Each track builds on the one previous; Tracks 2 and 3 are particularly experiential. The goal is most definitely *not* the training of teachers, leaders, and ministers who can then conduct good, content-rich programs back in the parish and finally make their small groups "work." The goal *is* individual empowerment, which leads to further empowerment of others, which leads to empowerment of still others in ever-widening circles. Let's see what it looks like when the process is in progress.

≈

The six women from St. T's spirituality committee thought they were in trouble; they were eager to be supplied with a few ideas or formats they could offer their parish. After all, the pastor named them and commissioned them; they had to start producing right after Christmas, but they weren't sure what the product should look like. Two of them were all for starting small groups. They liked what they had heard about base community and ecclesiola, or "little house church." Should they put an announcement in the bulletin and just start faith sharing with whomever showed up? What book should they use? With these anxieties motivating them, they signed up for Track 1 of "Greater Things...," hoping to learn something they could teach others, hoping to be exposed to some methods and models they could duplicate. They confessed a further worry; driving "all the way" to the center for ten successive weeks in late winter might prove harassing if not impossible. I agreed to drive the short distance to their parish hall where they were still more comfortable at this point.

These very good and generous individuals, eager to contribute something of their own substance to their church, provided a microcosmic view of the pervasive volunteer ministry mindset in the American church. The attitude includes a hunger for more life within the church, a desire to be instrumental in the change, coupled with a more subtle and passive demand that says, "Feed me the information I need; give me the tools; make it as comfortable as possible; keep the cost to the minimum, after all I'm doing this for you; I'll do my share of giving back but I'm too stressed out and overcommitted for more than that." The lay ministers themselves are not fully responsible for this mindset. They inherit this restrictive view of their possibilities from the tradition of a paternalistic, immigrant church whose self-avowed duty it was to provide all the religious, educational, and societal needs to people who could not provide these for themselves. The evolution from childhood through adolescence to the adulthood of the American church is still in progress.

≈

The evolution of this spirituality committee and eventually the parish of St. T's-in-the-City began this way. Because the groundwork of introducing spirituality to the parish had been laid in the preceding months, the actual process of this development resembled a flash of summer lightning rather than a gradual dawning. At our first Track 1 meeting, we gathered in a small, bare seminar room in St. T's basement. My six friends brought along the chairperson of the Baptismal Preparation Program, who wanted to "audit" the course. We began with a meditation adapted from *Prayers for a Planetary Pilgrim* by Edward Hays, which identified our own hoped-for spiritual evolution with the grand scale and ongoing birthing of the cosmos.[22] I acquainted them, that first evening, with ideas put forth by Fr. Gerry Broccolo in an address called "New Ways in Ministry," which he delivered to the Future of the American Church Conference (Time Consultants, Washington D.C. (September 17, 1988; audio and video cassettes available). Fr. Broccolo identifies and discusses shifts in the contemporary development of ministry: the *ground of ministry* as competence rather than role or lifestyle, the locus of *formation for ministry* as parish rather than seminary, and *spirituality for ministry* as wholistic rather than dualistic. Prior to investigating these three paradigmatic shifts, he establishes three constants in church ministry throughout history. I focused on the second of these, which is that ministry has constantly changed according to the pastoral needs of the individual time and place. It may seem paradoxical to identify change as a "constant," but that identification is essential for freeing people from the tyranny of the very recent past, the "we've *always* done it this way!" excuse for stagnation.

A brief overview of the two-millennia history of ecclesiology that I presented that evening was quite enough to make the spirituality committee gasp.

There was so much of the story of their own Tradition of which they had been unaware. Simply to hear that the term "laity" (*laos*, 1140 A.D.) was a relative newcomer to the Christian scene startled them. To begin to understand the term's implications for a class structure within the church that had everything to do with the development of feudalism in Western

Europe and nothing to do with the Acts of the Apostles was a perspective-shaking revelation.

Information that helps to situate clearly lay ministers, group leaders, or anyone else in their present moment as it *really* is — that is, the present as a natural step in an unfolding continuum that has both a past and a future — is the vital and primary but most often neglected element of preparation for ministry and the Christian life. More often, the focusing question in ministerial formation is "How do we do it?" and the response, "Here's how!" The really salient questions are "Who am I (are we)? Where did I (we) come from? Where am I (are we) going?" Any question that begs for the final word on the subject, any answer that intends closure, is antithetical to the *disclosure* of personal meaning. Without *informed* personal meaning, church-belonging as well as ministry are simply nice things to do on a Sunday morning or a Tuesday evening. The "doing" can be a comfortable excuse to avoid the painful mystery of "becoming." The "doing" confines me to the status of hireling; someone else's agenda and instructions are paramount for me. "Becoming" calls me toward the lived-out actualization of my Christed self as beloved daughter or son. I cannot "become" in a vacuum; I can only get by.

Since birthing rather than bandaiding is the operative image for ministry in the PARISH ALIVE! lexicon, Track 1 at St. T's was about *informed* becoming. For the next seven weeks we explored the stages of faith development according to Professor James Fowler. (An excellent eight-tape audio cassette series by Professor Fowler, including an instruction book, *Stages of Faith*, is available from Credence Cassettes. An abbreviated but clear and highly adequate description of the Fowler Faith Stages can be found in chapter 4 of *Christian Religious Education* by Thomas H. Groome, Harper & Row, 1980.)

Using a "shared praxis"[23] approach, wherein the participants' stories and visions enter into dialogue with the greater story and vision of the material and the Tradition to be productive of future praxis, we began this evening and all our remaining evenings together with a reflection question. Prayer focused on the Exodus event, and the question framed was this: "Israel's 'credo' (basic story) is about going out from a place and coming in to a new place. In your *basic story*, where have you come from, where are you going?" Written reflection and sharing on this question served to uncover the living movement of faith as journey, present and active in each participant.

As we began to look at Fowler's faith definition, members of the group could see similarities and differences in their own previously shared definitions, as well as the comparison of Fowler's definition with their own. We unpacked the five basic notions included in the Fowler definition: faith as primary, as active knowing, as relational, as rational and passional, as a human universal. The two most radical departures for the participants were Fowler's perception of faith as an action, a verb rather than a static thing possessed, and faith as more fundamental and broader than any particular religious expression of it. I found their disturbance a marvelously encouraging confirmation that calcified images were beginning to move and be shaken.

During the following weeks, we examined each of Fowler's six developmental stages of faith, noting that every stage of faith *is* faith. I placed a weighted emphasis on the crucial transition between Fowler's stage three, Synthetic/Conventional Faith, which arises during adolescence, and Fowler's stage four, Individuating/Reflexive Faith, which *may* originate in early adulthood. A person in stage three forms an acceptable synthesis among the various sources of authority in the "compartments" of his or her life. What "they" say is of paramount importance in the theater of my meaning and life. All authority resides outside myself and conventional wisdom is my guide. I find it essential to respond to those unlike myself with either prejudice and dismissal, or an urgent necessity to persuade them toward my own point of view and toward assimilation with my own group. My identity is still largely unformed and therefore I am unable to make independent judgments or to experience faith activity as self-chosen.

The dramatic leap from stage three to four begins to crystallize when the conventional synthesis starts to erode and weaken because of a perceived lack of "fit" between the external expectations of my various groups (family, community, church) and my real self. I begin to trust myself to take personal responsibility for my beliefs, values, attitudes, and commitments. To the extent that I grow through this stage, my stance toward both immediate and ultimate reality becomes more and more autonomous; to the same extent, my awareness of the paradoxes of life becomes more and more acute. My faith task takes the form of an inner dialogue between the paradoxical elements, without succumbing again to the temptation of an "either-or" position and consequent return to stage three patterns of living and relating to God, myself, and others.

To the extent that I am able to embrace a "both-and" attitude through continued individuation and reflection, I am preparing to move to stage five, which Fowler calls Conjunctive Faith. Stage five reflects a willingness to live with questions that open inward and point to deeper questions, an embrace of old verities in new ways, an active and committed concern for the whole of humanity, not simply for those who do it my way.

Stage six, Universalizing Faith, is the condition of living that Christians might call sainthood. A person who functions on this level of faith ceases to be the central reference point for reality and lives and acts in a constant awareness of Divine Presence immanent in every creature and permeating all of creation. Such a person both cherishes life passionately and holds life as lightly as dust upon the open palm of the hand.

It was noted throughout our discussions that these faith stages tend to overlap, particularly during transitional periods. For example, particularities common to stages one and two, the proper developmental phases of faith in early and middle childhood, may endure, requiring recognition and attention during any of the successive stages. Participants came to realize that in leading small faith-sharing groups, they would meet people in all these stages of faith development. They grasped the importance of recognizing the stages and reverencing other individuals' positions. In the past, with this developmental reality still unnamed, they had feared falling prey to polemics that would arise in faith groups, which they believed would flow from members' disagreement with the "truth." Now their own consciousnesses were expanding their comprehension of the leader's role from question-answerer or problem-solver to "pilgrim with."

Two other realities that began to take shape for them were intimately related. In a special moment of clarity, one participant reflected what the others suspected. "It seems probable to me that although stage three faith begins somewhere around junior high, many people remain in that stage until they die! Even though they develop a brilliant career or reach the pinnacle of success in their field, some folks never attain more than a 'pray, pay, and obey' pattern in their faith dimension!" She had perfectly described the trap of "cultural Catholicism" wherein interior spiritual struggle, growth in autonomy of faith in action and development of inclusive community are never necessary. Stage three faith, of course, is not denominational; if faith is, as Fowler claims, a human universal, then a person of any Tradition may be tied to an external faith system for a lifetime and may never recognize the root cataclysm of invitation to the crucial transition as anything more than "mid-life crisis."

The mega-reality paralleling the personal faith journey that is so easily truncated at stage three is the centuries-long faith journey of the global Christian consciousness. Participants at St. T's took a look at the corporate Person of Christianity, the Body of Christ, moving not through years but through centuries, to our point in time when the continued existence of the Christian churches hangs in the balance. Coming to light throughout the second half of the twentieth century is the whole-church transition from stage three to four. Sparks flew as this understanding emerged for the little group in the church basement; excitement mounted as they perceived themselves as midwives to a newborn faith-level life in their own local cell of the universal church. Their role was both simpler and infinitely more profound than they had imagined. But still they were primarily task-oriented.

And then, at one session, it happened! A certain gentle participant made a shy and trembling intervention. "Is it possible, through learning all this, which is quite wonderful, that I myself, that we ourselves, might begin to move from one level of faith to another? That's what I really want!" Fireworks! Music! Applause!

When the group leader in training or the head of a parish ministry or the catechist or the pastor consciously acknowledges herself or himself as one on a journey who does what she or he does *with* others rather than *for* others, we have arrived at the starting point of limitless life for that group or that parish. When that one participant named and claimed her real desire, her trembling arose not from any anxiety but from the sudden illumination of self-knowledge and interior meaning. The others in the group experienced a resonance with her words and her feelings and began to express, each in her own way, a related personal reality. The spirituality committee came into being that evening. The circle in which they sat seemed to be a mandala with Christ as center point. The Sanskrit word *mandala* means to be in possession of one's essence.

Throughout Track 1 we had often examined several approaches to critical faith issues. As the group's knowledge of the stages of faith developed, they found it increasingly easier to determine which approach originated in each of the six stages. They were becoming more adept in finding ways to receive each approach, and they would respectfully draw and challenge the speaker to consider an alternative approach on a deeper level.

Two other spiritual directors, my colleagues at the center, came to St. T's for the final sessions of Track 1 to share the "Art of Dialogue" with the spirituality committee. The "Art" begins with interior prayer when I become aware of my inner space that receives the Other, when the truth of who I am meets the truth of who God is. Scripture passages were used. The participants placed themselves within the stories and received the words of Jesus. They used the listening skills of mind, heart, and body to receive the truth of the Word. The intentionality of one who practices the art of dialogue rests on the premise that for the speaker whatever she says is, for her, the truth; the listener agrees to receive it as such. Within such a dialogue where speaking and listening achieve mutuality, a new truth evolves. Insofar as the art of dialogue exists in a person's prayer, the same style is reflected in interpersonal faith communication in the human community. Judgment and correction are transformed by the dialoguing facilitator of the faith group into receptivity and mutuality.

Enter the great surprise! Before Track 1 was completed, the chairperson of the spirituality committee informed me that the group had formally decided to meet one Sunday a month in one another's homes to experience what it is to be a faith-sharing group. (This would become a weekly meeting when Track 1 ended.) They would each alternate as facilitators. Their first meeting produced a unanimous desire to let the parish know of their existence, in which they themselves now delighted. Individual members or pairs of members were considering facilitating six-week seminars and other offerings with which they were already familiar. Two members of the committee had also opted to receive individual monthly direction from a qualified spiritual director. Not nearly at the end, but right in the middle of their learning, the confidence of transformed consciousness was impelling them from within toward empowerment of others.

Still somewhat reticent, the chairperson suggested next September as a good time to begin the "seminars." My counter-suggestion grew out of the actually lived life of St. T's; as a parish of exquisite liturgical capability, they had just celebrated the Sacred Triduum with such beauty that their parish was being praised throughout the diocese. Why not touch into this rightful pride of identity right now, in the Eastertime? After all, the academic year is really not the appropriate model for the ecclesial life cycle. How about inviting St. T's to mystagogia?

"Mistah Who?" asked my friend, the chairperson. "Mystagogia" is the ancient ecclesial celebration and living out of the Easter mysteries in which we participate annually, but develop in explanation and practice throughout the rest of the year.

The spirituality committee developed an attractive spring-green flier called "Seasons of Celebration at St. T's" to be distributed to every parishioner with the church bulletin on a late April weekend. The heading extended this invitation: "The Spirituality Team at St. T's invites you to consider these possibilities for dynamic spiritual growth! Why not be really good to yourself and allow the Easter Mysteries of new life and community, which we have just celebrated together, to come alive in your life across the seasons?" Beneath this was a drawing of the empty tomb, and the words in the margin proclaimed life to be lived in spring, summer, fall and winter. A six-week segment, "Coming Alive in Faith" (an experience with which four of the leaders' group were already familiar, having served on the parish team for a previous Isaiah 43 Mission), was to be offered once in the late spring and once in the fall. A parish retreat day, completely planned and presented by members of the spirituality team and called "Welcome Summer," was to be offered in June. "Pray," a program by Richard Huelsman, SJ (Paulist Press, 1976), would be offered weekly from September through December. This vehicle, which develops a Gospel-oriented approach to daily life, a deeper prayer life with practice in scriptural meditation, and a very powerful impetus toward small faith communities, was more than familiar to the committee's chairperson, who had, some years before, experienced her own adult conversion at a distant parish while a participant in "Pray." She had later adapted the material for use with teenagers.

"Seasons of Celebration at St. T's" also offered Track 2 of "Greater Things...," which I would present at the center in the fall; not so surprisingly, everyone who participated in Track 1 now saw the distance to the center as short indeed! Newcomers for Track 1 would also be welcome. The green flier announced an "Evening of Spirituality" in November, entitled "Harvest of Faith." A parishioner trained in spirituality had agreed to present that offering; as the mother of five small boys she had much experience to blend with her knowledge. "Advent Mornings," which I planned to offer again at the center in December, rounded out the seasonal invitations and continued to extend the center itself as a resource to parishioners.

Do you see now that those six women always had known "how" and "what"? Their courage and creativity had been let loose because now they were more in touch with "who" they were and "who" they wished to become.

The June day arrived for St. T's Parish Retreat Day, "Welcome Summer," at the Center by the Sea. I was scheduled to serve as center hostess that weekend. The spirituality team had hoped for fifteen registrations for this day that they had so meticulously planned as a "Journey to Emmaus" and had so deeply prepared for in prayer. Forty-five of their sister and brother parishioners arrived. Among the participating retreatants was the pastor of St.T's. I was awed but not at all surprised as I watched the day unfold from my place on the sidelines. These women had created from their own personal and parish resources a day of power and peace, a day that was fully alive! Elements of experiential prayer and ritual, meditation, presentations and facilitated faith sharing all had a place. The pastor, sitting in the third row, was overwhelmed with glad emotion as he witnessed his parishioners empowering other parishioners, inviting them to more life, greater depth, the recognition of the Christ in the broken bread of their ordinary lives. This man, may I remind you, was one of the ten pastors who had accepted our invitation to "Come and See" just nine months before this June retreat day. He looked and believed and saw the full circle coming round.

Late that afternoon, the volunteer who operates our Center Creative Gift and Bookstore was already gone for the day when I received a number of requests from St. T's people who wished to buy books. I decided to reopen the store, which quickly filled with about two dozen people on a break. Standing behind the counter, I overheard one young woman on line asking another which books she was purchasing. Much impressed by her companion's three titles in spirituality, she commented, "Oh, you must be very involved in the church!" "Actually," came the response, "I hadn't been to church since I was a kid, until recently. I took a six-week seminar from the spirituality committee at the parish and I felt a sort of explosion inside me. Now all I want to do is learn more and participate more. It feels like I just can't get enough, like I've been starving for a long time without knowing it. This thing that's happening at St. T's, it's all part of something called PARISH ALIVE! I don't really know what that is, or where it came from, but who cares? All I know is *I'm* alive!" It was her turn now to pay for the books. "How much for these books, ma'am?" she inquired pleasantly. The young woman had no idea why my answering smile was so broad!

When St. T's spirituality team arrives at the center for Track 2 of "Greater Things...," they will expect five two-hour sessions of practice at "Facilitation of Faith Sharing Groups." Other participants in Track 2 from different parishes will join with them, including a group from St. P's Episcopal Church. The content will be brief at each evening's session, because each participant will have a turn at facilitating a period of small-group sharing. A variety of materials will be used and it will be stressed that the materials are arbitrary and should be chosen according to the thrust of life in their parish.

Some examples of materials are *Pray*, by Richard Huelsman, SJ, for a parish most desiring an emphasis on meditation and Scripture; *Mission Evangelization*, by Robert Deshaies et al., in a parish whose central work is the evangelization of the unchurched in their area; *A Third Look at Jesus*, by Carlos H. Abesamis, in a parish whose overarching concern is mutuality with the third world poor; *Prayer Course for Healing Life's Hurts*, by Matthew and Dennis Linn and Sheila Fabricant, in a parish whose healing ministry is paramount; *Coming Home: A Handbook for Exploring Sanctuary Within*, by Betsy Caprio and Thomas M. Hedberg, where the interplay of psychology and spirituality is important; *Praying Alone and Praying Together*, by Art Baranowski where the primary energy of the parish is being expended to restructure unto small faith communities; *The Star in My Heart: Experiencing Sophie, Inner Wisdom*, by Joyce Rupp, where extrovert meditation through creative arts is appropriate; *Take and Receive Series: A Guide for Prayer*, by Jacqueline Syrup Bergan and S. Marie Schwan, where there is sustained interest in the Ignatian Spiritual Exercises.

All these publications, and many others, provide either facilitators' manuals or instructions in the basic text for multiweek group meetings. They are simply thematic vehicles around which to employ the old Christian strategy that says gather the folks, tell the stories, and break the bread. *This* bread, which is the substance of our very lives, becomes the sustenance for the life of our friends.

A collegial critique of each small-group session's effectiveness, at the end of Track 2 evenings, will provide an experience of group supervision. The instructor's role for Track 2 is to put forth simple guiding principles for faith-group facilitators, to introduce a wide range of effective materials, to create an atmosphere conducive to confidence and collegiality, and to encourage creative choices appropriate to specific local situations. The rationale for Track 2 is practical experience in facilitation of small groups, with guidance.

Later in the year, Track 3 will convene at the center for eight weeks to acquaint lay parish ministers with the age-old ecclesial role of one-to-one spiritual companioning and to begun to equip them with some necessary skills for this role. Not every person back in the home parish will have the need or inclination to establish a relationship with a professional qualified director, but more and more people *are* seeking an able companion for their personal spiritual journey. This companion (literally, one who breaks bread together with me) must be someone who is also growing in the interior life and has developed an acuity in listening to the movements of the human heart.

Spiritual companioning is already practiced informally and in an unnamed way every time two Christians sit down over coffee in a neighborhood kitchen to talk about meaning in their lives, the stirrings of God within them, or their hunger for a more personal connection to Jesus Christ. Most lay ministers who will come to Track 3 have already had the experience of people in the parish seeking them out for spiritual "advice." The two basic components of Track 3, directed reading (see the annotated bibliography in Appendix 2) and role play for the spiritual companion, will supply them with background information and skill practice. Weekly and varied prayer experiences that model both extroverted and introverted preferences for prayer will put them in touch with a variety of prayer styles that they may encourage for the spectrum of personalities with which they will deal.

Titles on the directed reading list include classic and specifically contemporary treatments of one-to-one spiritual companioning. Each participant will be responsible for one book and commentary on it, including the surfacing of relevant discussion questions that arise from the text for the gathered group of aspiring spiritual companions. Role play will require participants to pair off, one as spiritual companion, the other as parishioner seeking companioning for the struggle with specific spiritual life issues. Ten-to-fifteen-minute role-play sessions will be viewed by the whole group and then critiqued.

Track 3, specializing in precise and delicate skills, requires facilitation by a certified experienced professional spiritual director. It is essential therefore for those groups desiring a Track 3 component to make contact with such a person at a local retreat center or to be put in touch with a list of qualified spiritual directors through a local diocesan office.

Participants in Track 3 will be urged to consider regular spiritual direction for themselves, if they have not already done so. The best spiritual companions for others will be those who have their own ongoing experience of receiving personal and careful direction. They will come to understand by experience how to hold the spiritual journey agenda of another with reverence, compassion, confidentiality, and discernment.

"Whoever believes in me will perform the same works as I do myself, that person will do even greater things than I..." (John 14:12).

Tracks 1, 2, and 3 ask this: Are you interested in maintaining a parish and its activities or are you interested in birthing the reign of God?

· 9 ·

IN YOUR MIDST ...

You HAVE EVERYTHING you need within you to begin to bring
your own person and your own parish alive! The seed of human
transformation is that still, small voice inside that says only
one word, "More!" Very much like the mustard seed, your seed
of desire for more life can grow to become a noble shade tree to
shelter and give a home place to so many others on their way.

If you have used your imagination to allow what you have
read in this book to be reclothed in the circumstances of your
own locale, you have taken the first step. If you have dreamed
of your own possibilities, suggested by reading these pages, with
just one other parishioner, you have taken a second step. Have
you phoned the pastor and made an appointment to discuss the
need you and other parishioners feel for some experience and
knowledge in the area of spirituality? Has he suggested that
he will get in touch with the diocesan office, to check out resources, personnel, and materials? Ah, yes! Soon you will be
dancing!

Listen to the music. Let your inner eye penetrate the future
for just a moment; yes, you can see your own parish hall transformed by the rising morning star. You can see a place of holy
hospitality, a pilgrim inn, where small groups of people speak
and breathe and live the Good News together. You can feel a
surge of power as human, divine, and natural interconnectivity
expand your capacity for daily living. Yes, you can almost smell
your grandmother's soup simmering on the stove, this place is
that much like "home."

Your vision begins to melt now, so overshadowed is it by
the passion you feel for more life. The walls of the parish hall
have become so transparent, the veil so thin. There is nothing
that can stop you and the others from going forth into the city
to tell what you have seen and heard. The structure can no
longer contain you, the very earth is alive with grace beneath
your feet. A new phase of the church is coming into being,
with your agreement and your energy as its lifeblood. All you
need to do is say yes to the Beloved who lives within you and
begin the first step of the dance. The Beloved will teach you
the rest.

When Fr. Bob and I completed our ministry report at the
end of the first nine months of PARISH ALIVE!, we saw that
our little yellow "mustard seed" brochure had put us into
formal, presentational contact with 1,982 parish persons in
that brief time period. We realized that the ripples-in-the-
pond dynamic had probably increased the numerical impact
of PARISH ALIVE! substantially. But we were never interested in
numbers, so the actual figure is unimportant. What *was* important to us was the verification of the serious hunger for
spirituality that we more than suspected exists in the local
church.

Equally important was the comparative ease and simplicity with which people had accepted new master images of
God, Self, and Others, old truths renamed, wholistic spirituality, classic prayer forms to which they had never been exposed,
ritual that is perceived not only rationally but sensibly, expanded sense of personal mission, faith-sharing at deep levels
of the true self...and the list goes on. The evidence was over-
whelming in that first year of PARISH ALIVE! that parishioners
personally empowered in their own spirituality were perfectly
capable and profoundly willing to empower others, allowing the
ordinary local parish to begin to grow organically as a spiritual
life center. We decided to continue to work with the original ten
parishes on a consultative basis during the second year and to

choose six additional parishes to "Come and See." The ripples had already spread from pond to stream; pastors were calling us before we had a chance to dial their numbers. The pieces of the puzzle were beginning to interlock.

≈

What are your own local spirituality resources? Do you as a parishioner, a parish, or a diocese have the possibility of interfacing with an established retreat house, where qualified spiritual directors are at work? Is there a Carmel or other monastery nearby where someone may be an experienced teacher of spirituality? Is there an area college with a reputable religious studies faculty with whom you might get in contact? Have you asked your diocesan office of spirituality or evangelization if they have a listing of small local houses of prayer, which are now springing up from Long Island to Florida to Illinois to California? Most of them are directed by people with degrees in spirituality and certified in spiritual direction. (Please make sure you check credentials!) Do you have a diocesan media resource center connected with religious education or parish renewal? Most of these centers function as lending libraries for a small annual parish fee. Examples have been noted throughout this book of stunning audiovisual materials that are perfect for content input in the absence of a spirituality professional.

If you are the director of a retreat center, might you consider an offer of collaboration with your local diocese? If you are a pastor, a bishop, or a diocesan vicar in the area of spirituality or renewal, might you consider linking with spirituality resources in your area of jurisdiction on behalf of the people you serve? In our diocese, officially stated collaboration with the center became grace and blessing on the parochial level.

≈

PARISH ALIVE! invites everyone and anyone to initiate the dance. The steps will vary from place to place but the dancing partners and the music remain the same. Human transformation and spirituality are bound together, waiting for the music of Ruah to begin — Ruah, the Spirit of God who broods over creation and in the depths of each human spirit, waiting to be invited to play.

Appendix 1

ECUMENICAL IMPLICATIONS FOR PARISH ALIVE!

During the first year of the PARISH ALIVE! process as it took place in the Roman Catholic diocese of Providence, R.I. I was privileged to participate in a doctor of ministry in spiritual direction program of the Graduate Theological Foundation (Donaldson, Ind.). My forty-seven colleagues in the program came from a diversity of Christian traditions as well as a broad geographical base. Most of my colleagues were ordained within their Tradition; many of them had additional degrees in psychology, spirituality, administration, sociology, or education.

As pastoral professionals from traditions that most often have *not* included the dimensions of spirituality and/or spiritual direction, it is noteworthy that they were pursuing and have since been granted the advanced ministerial degree in spiritual direction. The unanimous consensus among my colleagues was that a church without an explicit blossoming of personal and communal spirituality is a church that will not survive the transition into the next century.

I queried my colleagues concerning their lived-out, personal, pastoral-professional experience of the relationship between "parish" and "spirituality." The following comments represent responses from eight different Christian traditions. This sample suggests the hunger and possibility for PARISH ALIVE! process across the ecumenical spectrum.

123

Rev. Howard F. Kempsell, Jr., Rector, Christ Church Parish
(Episcopal), Plymouth, Massachusetts:

The parish is the locus of spirituality for most Episcopalians.
Some of our folks complement or supplement the spiritual nurture they receive beyond the local congregation, but those, I
think, would be in the minority.

Anglicans (of which the Episcopal Church, U.S.A., is one
branch) have always valued Scripture, Tradition, and reason
(experience reflected upon) as sources of authority in spiritual formation. Today, it seems that fewer and fewer of our
members are engaged in any regular, serious Bible Study. And
where church history (Tradition) is studied, the ascetical and
mystical traditions are bypassed. Thus, what we have is a
crisis in spiritual formation, from the Anglican perspective,
wherein reason/personal experience becomes the sole determin-
ing factor in moral decision making. Many of our folks are
cut off from their spiritual roots and don't know what they
are missing. Perhaps they think of themselves as flourishing,
but in reality they may be more akin to artificial greenery:
It looks pretty for a time; then the color begins to fade. It
can never support life, its own or another's. Happy will be
the day when the two legs of Scripture and Tradition are restored to our, at present, one-legged stool. I see my role as
priest and spiritual director as becoming so steeped in Scripture and Tradition that, in a very important sense, I become
an incarnation of what I am trying to communicate. This is
no small task, but by the grace of God I will continue with the
vision.

Rev. Joseph Newcomer, Minister, First Congregational Church
(United Church of Christ), Nampa, Idaho:

The parish should be a center of spirituality. It should be a
place where spiritual growth is the order of the day. The life of
each person should be a point of intersection of spirituality and
the parish: this is my hope and dream.

Dr. Joseph H. Hagan, President, Assumption College,
Worcester, Massachusetts; Immaculate Conception Parish,
Assumption College Worshiping Community:

The concepts of parish and spirituality must necessarily inter-
act. If Christians do not receive the basics of spirituality in the
parish setting, they may never receive them. It is the obligation
of pastors to see that spiritual concerns are actively promoted
within the parish.

George L. Cumberbatch, Pastor, First Baptist Church,
Freeport, Grand Bahamas:

For me, spirituality involves the deepening of my spiritual life
with God; it's a journey inward that includes a life of contemplative prayer, meditation and fasting, etc. The journey
continues outward in my relationship in a God-like way to the
world around me; the developing God within me, my inner self,
does the latter. Paul speaks of it in terms of "Christ living in
me" and I add "through me." I feel that all believers of the
body, the parish, should have spirituality as their goal. I find,
however, that most of them (my congregation) are minimal believers; they have no desire to go beyond the initial Christian
experience. The quest for greater spiritually is viewed, it seems,
with fear and suspicion. There are but a few exceptions to this
observation. It appears that a majority of folks come to church
for other reasons and are content to remain marginal in their
spirituality. Nominalism seems to be more the order of the day.

Rev. George J. Cramer, D.Min., Director of Ministry
Formation, Diocese (Roman Catholic) of Jefferson City,
Missouri:

I perceive the parish as more the generic place of spiritual development—more the social lubricant condition, the milieu, in
which a person gathers a sense of place (a past, a present, and
a future) and a life/faith trajectory. The parish is the situation

in which one's faith journey is publicly ritualized/liturgized/manifested/affirmed/sustained/evaluated/transformed. In our culture, I perceive the spiritual journey as a more personal response to a perceived "call" from one's "divine" (God?). The parish seems to be the situation in which a person is sustained/supported through the journey — especially by those in the community who have already traversed the route, as well as those presently struggling along within it. Spirituality would be a personal response. Parish would be a milieu of nurture — not absolutely necessary in the journey, but helpful (ideally, the parish would be the place of nurture par excellence).

Rev. Winter V. Lantz, Consultant, Presbyterian Church, U.S.A.,
Orlando, Florida:

In practice, the life of the parish, with its heavy emphasis on programs, content, relationships, finances, leaves little room for satisfying the spiritual yearning of individuals. Opportunities for true spirit centered community are few and are often carried by a few "on-fire" persons. How can we be still with so much parish activity? I suspect the Spirit won't sit still long enough to be programmed; in depth spiritual development will take place at the edges. The "gentle pressure of the will" insures that this will be so.

Rev. James R. Stuck, St. Paul Lutheran Church,
Michigan City, Indiana:

Basically, our parish understands spiritual development as something that happens to young people. Through our Sunday School, Confirmation program, Christian Day School, etc., these young people will develop their faith, which will keep them in good standing (with a few good works) for the rest of their lives. Spiritual development stops at Grade 8 with Confirmation. Also, spirituality is something very private; you don't talk about it. It is between you and God. Public worship is to be formal and optional. Personal spiritual life is to be private. Prayer is usually an embarrassing practice if made public.

Dr. Daniel Paul Vincent, Deacon, St. Paul the Apostle Parish (Roman Catholic), New Orleans, Louisiana:

The spiritual life of St. Paul's exists in different forms and within a loose network of small groups. My sense of the situation is that the pastor and the members of the individual groups have a totally different concept of what spirituality is. The majority of the congregation's notions of spirituality most likely are rooted in remembrances of the Baltimore Catechism. Through my ministry, I have come to believe that the people need and want more spiritual direction. The challenge is for the pastor and congregation to seek and hopefully find a common ground that will result in spiritual awakening and growth at both the community and individual levels.

Ann Kulp, Church Educator and Consultant, National Capital Presbytery, Washington, D.C.; Consultant on Referral Staff of Shalem Institute for Spiritual Formation:

My perception of "spirituality" in the Presbyterian Church and ten-year experience in the United Church of Christ is that it is: (a) not often used as a term, so understanding is very limited, (b) a term implying mystery and in some cases mysticism, and may sound scary, certainly not biblical, (c) taken for granted because the root word is "spirit" and worship is spiritual, so what more do we need? (d) an offshoot of something Roman Catholic, so we do not recognize it as part of our heritage, misnomer though that is, (e) okay, if you speak of spiritual growth, spiritual renewal, or spiritual enrichment; the concept 'spirituality' is vague and foreign, (f) in demand within the subconscious, if not the conscious mind of a majority of parishioners who do not know how to name or nurture their hunger for God beyond the traditional church pew. That is why I feel called to work within the organized church, specifically to respond to the need Howard Thurman identifies as 'Deep is the Hunger.'"

Rev. Paul Hanneman, Pastor, Immanuel Baptist Church (American Baptist), Portland, Maine:

Immanuel called me to be their pastor because they wanted to grow spiritually. By this, I believe they meant that the institutional aspect of the parish was going well, but they knew they needed a deeper spiritual foundation for community and ministry. In the two years since my coming, we have begun to work on deepening spirituality, both in individual guidance and in a developing corporate sense of God's call. Within the Protestant free church tradition, there is little sense of cultivating the inner life; thus, programs and preaching on its reality, and the practice of attending to the Presence of God Within, have been of an introductory nature.

The Rev. Dr. Pat Seymour, Interim Rector, St. Paul's Episcopal Church, Lansing, Michigan:

I view parish and spirituality as dependent on one another. Parish is a place where we ordinary folk can see ourselves on a Spiritual Journey of even closer times with God in Christ Jesus through the power of the Holy Spirit. My hope is that more and more people will see themselves on a holy adventure. Parish is, of necessity, a place of flexible people. Calling for real spirituality in a parish is often a radical but welcome departure in the life of that parish — for ordinary folk.

I experience spirituality in the parish in relationships and in people's relationships with God. The clergy can invite all people on a spiritual journey and then listen, as well as preach. The preacher/homilist can radiate the love of Jesus Christ over and over again. Where conflict exists, only spiritual healing can resolve it.

Sister Margaret Mary Moloney, RSM, Spiritual Director,
St. Thomas the Apostle Parish (Roman Catholic),
Naperville, Illinois:

If we are agreed that spiritual hunger exists among parishioners in our various parishes today, then undoubtedly the
parish is the most appropriate place to fill this ever-growing
need. A parish that lacks a strong emphasis on a life
lived out of Gospel values usually represents a "Mass-on-
Sunday" mentality, with finances, and other administrative
problems consuming much of the leadership time in the parish. Matters of peace and justice, concern for the poor and
needy, and organized ministries are not uppermost in such
institutions.

On the other hand, where pastor and staff are deeply committed to a faith-filled community of God's people, spirituality
becomes a top priority, evidenced in liturgies, programs, and
ministries. If a parish believes that the kingdom of God is
now, then ministers, staff, and parishioners become holy people, demonstrating their eager desire to bring about change as
followers of Christ.

Lynn E. Spitz-Nagel, Pastor, Faith Church
(United Church of Christ), Matteson, Illinois:

Spirituality, spiritual renewal, must be integrated thoroughly
into the life of the church/parish. Over the long haul, spiritual
renewal will come in the places and times where the church/
parish already gathers regularly — worship, learning time, service, decision making, budget, fellowship times, in our caring
for each other — and will happen as we deepen the quality of
our experiences in those times and places. The biblical images
and the sacramental experiences of the gathered community
have the power to awaken a fuller and deeper relationship with
the God revealed in Jesus Christ.

John R. Simmons, Pastor, Mayfair Christian Church
(Disciples of Christ), Stockton, California:

Parish — Spirituality...How do they connect? I love administration, but too often, administration is form without substance; so the trick is to have administration flow out of substance. Spirituality is the connection in people with themselves, each other, and God, in the action of the parish. Spirituality is not form; it is the recognition and constant allowance for the interconnectedness between us in the work of the parish from study, kitchen, sanctuary, soup kitchen, to the polls.

The Rev. Sarah B. Taylor, Associate Pastor,
First Presbyterian Church,
Rockaway, New Jersey:

I believe that everything true in the parish *can* be undergirded and guided by a deep sense of the spiritual, namely, the presence of God and Christ in the midst of all that is done. We strive to do this by making the parish Christ's parish, by prayer and devotions at all "business" meetings, as well as studies; by Christ-centered worship; by providing a variety of ways to experience God in one's life: worship, Bible study, contemplative and meditative prayer groups, spiritually centered retreats for officers, music, etc.

As we become more centered, it is obvious in the living warmth, the creative ministry (of all, lay persons included), the inner peace that keeps our frantic schedule together, and in the drawing of new people to the church. And of course, by reminding ourselves and all others that the journey always continues and broadens, even as it deepens. Therefore, it encourages questions and growth in faith development, by Christ's love, God's grace, and the *living presence* of the Spirit."

*Jack O'Keefe, Lay Minister, St. Francis Cathedral
(Roman Catholic), Santa Fe, New Mexico:*

Parish and spirituality generally do not intersect. Because of limited clergy, untrained laity, and fear of ambiguity, we muddle along, stifling personal growth in favor of the status quo. If the parish of the twenty-first century is to flourish, parish and spirituality must be one.

Appendix 2

SUGGESTED DIRECTED READING LIST

For Track 3 of "Greater Things..." (chapter 8)

Barry, William A., and William J. Connolly. *The Practice of Spiritual Direction*. San Francisco: Harper & Row Publishers, 1982. Preeminent contemporary classic.

Carmody John. *Toward a Male Spirituality*. Mystic, Conn.: Twenty-Third Publications, 1989. Stresses a theological as well as an emotionally informed approach to masculine spirituality.

Dyckman, Katherine Marie, and Patrick Carroll, SJ. *Inviting the Mystic, Supporting the Prophets: An Introduction to Spiritual Direction*. New York: Paulist Press, 1981. Offers encouragement and practical suggestions to those involved in spiritual companioning.

Edwards, Tilden. *Spiritual Friend: Reclaiming the Gift of Spiritual Direction*. New York/Ramsey: Paulist Press, 1980. The special friendship of support and guidance that one Christian can give to another over time; practical considerations for the spiritual companion by the director of Shalem Institute for Spiritual Formation.

Ferder, Fran. *Words Made Flesh: Scripture, Psychology and Human Communication*. Note Dame, Ind.: Ave Maria Press, 1986. The psychology of human interaction and communication related to the Gospel.

Fiand, Barbara. *Releasement: Spirituality for Ministry*. New York: Crossroad, 1987. Concerns the attitude, necessary for ministry, of creative surrender to mystery working itself out in our lives and the lives of others.

Finley, James. *The Awakening Call: Fostering Intimacy with God*. Notre Dame, Ind.: Ave Maria Press, 1984. Finley shares his own inner journey; a personal record of movement toward contemplative spirituality.

Fischer, Kathleen R. *The Inner Rainbow: The Imagination in Christian Life*. New York: Paulist Press, 1983. How to help others evoke and heal their master images of God, Self, and Others.

———. *Women at the Well: Feminist Perspective on Spirituals Direction*. New York/Mahwah: Paulist Press, 1988.

Fleming, David L., SJ. *Notes on the Spirituals Exercises of St. Ignatius of Loyola*. The Best of the Review, vol. 1. St. Louis, Mo.: Review for Religious, 1987.

———, ed. *The Christian Ministry of Spiritual Direction*. The Best of the Review, vol. 3. St. Louis: Review for Religious, 1988. Classic Jesuit treatment of the topic.

Keating, Dr. Charles J. *Who We Are Is How We Pray: Matching Personality and Spirituality*. Mystic, Conn.: Twenty-Third Publications, 1987.

Kelsey, Morton T. *Prophetic Ministry: The Psychology and Spirituality of Pastoral Care*. New York: Crossroad, 1982. A call to reawaken the forgotten ministry of spiritual guidance among others.

Michael, Chester P., and Marie C. Norrisey. *Prayer and Temperament: Different Prayer Forms for Different Personality Types*. Charlottesville, Va.: The Open Door, 1984.

O'Collins, Gerald. *The Second Journey*. New York/Ramsey: Paulist Press, 1978. Understanding core issues of mid-life.

Pable, Martin W., O.F.M. Cap. *A Man and His God*. Notre Dame, Ind.: Ave Maria Press, 1988. Draws on Tradition, Scripture, and contemporary psychology to develop a Gospel-centered spirituality that connects with men's contemporary issues.

Seiner, Edward C. *Mentoring: The Ministry of Spiritual Kinship*. Notre Dame, Ind.: Ave Maria Press, 1990. A new and vital understanding of the ancient Christian ideas concerning spiritual companionship.

Whitehead, Evelyn Eaton, and James D. Whitehead. *Seasons of Strength: New Visions of Adult Christian Maturing*. New York: Doubleday Image Books, 1984. Practical reflection on the stages, paths, and images of adult Christian maturing.

NOTES

Chapter 3: Spirituality for the Edge of an Age

✓ 1. "Song Over the Waters," *Shepherd Me, O God* (Chicago: GIA Publications, Inc., 1987).

✓ 2. Walter Brueggemann, et al., *To Act Justly, Love Tenderly, Walk Humbly* (Mahwah, N.J.: Paulist Press, 1986), 5.

3. Felicia McKnight, "Until the Morning Star," 1985.

4. "Servant Song," Rory Cooney, *Mystery* (Phoenix: North American Liturgy Resources, 1987).

5. "Each Winter As the Year Grows Older," Marty Haugen, © 1971 by United Church Press, Philadelphia, *Night of Silence* (Chicago: GIA Publications, Inc., 1987).

✓ 6. Matthew Fox, *Meditations with Meister Eckhart: A Centering Book* (Santa Fe, N.M.: Bear & Company, Inc., 1983), 78–81.

7. Gerald May, "Changeless and Calm," in *Sound Faith: Chants Used at the Shalem Institute* (Washington, D.C.: Isabella Bates, 2303 Chain Bridge Road, N.W., Washington, DC 20016, 1989).

✓ 8. Thomas Keating, *Open Mind, Open Heart: The Contemplative Dimension of the Gospel* (Warwick, N.Y.: Amity House, 1986), 19.

Chapter 5: Come Aside and Rest Awhile/Take Two

9. Joe Motta, "PARISH ALIVE! Enhances Parish Spirituality by Focusing on Individuals," *Providence Visitor*, March 28, 1991, 5.

Chapter 6: One in Mind and Heart

✓ 10. "New Ways of Understanding Ministry," Rev. Gerard Broccolo at the Future of the American Church Conference, Washington, D.C., September 17, 1988. Audio and video cassettes available from

Chesapeake Audiovideo Communications, Inc., 6330 Howard Lane, Elkridge, MD 21227.

11. "Whose Side Is God On?," *Westerly* (R.I.) *Sun*, editorial page, January 22, 1991.

12. *Ritual Songs*, Salina Star, Rt. Gold Hill, Boulder, CO 80302, audio cassette.

13. Martin Buber, *I and Thou: A New Translation by Walter Kaufmann* (New York: Charles Scribner's Sons, 1970), 168.

14. Bruce Bochte, ed., *Canticle to the Cosmos*, study guide, vol. 5 with Brian Swimme (San Francisco: Tides Foundation, 1990), editor's note.

15. Thomas Berry, "Twelve Principles," *Thomas Berry and the New Cosmology*, ed. Anne Lonergan and Caroline Richards (Mystic, Conn.: Twenty-Third Publications, 1987), 107.

16. Ibid., 108.

Chapter 7: Season of Refreshment

17. Walter Brueggemann, *The Prophetic Imagination* (Philadelphia: Fortress Press, 1978), 13.

18. David Steindl-Rast, *Gratefulness the Heart of Prayer* (Ramsey, N.J.: Paulist Press, 1984), 127.

19. Fran Ferder, *Words Made Flesh* (Notre Dame: Ave Maria Press, 1986), 31–48.

20. Christopher Fry, *A Sleep of Prisoners* (New York, London: Oxford University Press, 1957), 47–48.

21. St. Louis Jesuits "Who Are We O Lord?" *The Steadfast Love*, vol. 2. (Phoenix: North American Liturgy Resources, 1985).

Chapter 8: Greater Things Than I Shall You Do...

22. Edward Hays, "Destination: Planet Emmaus," *Prayers for a Planetary Pilgrim* (Easton, Kans.: Forest of Peace Books, 1988), 287–89.

23. Thomas H. Groome, *Christian Religious Education* (New York: Harper & Row, 1980). Chap. 9, "Shared Christian Praxis," 184–206, and chap. 10, "Praxis in Praxis," 208–32, provide Groome's principles and methodology for specific praxis approaches in a variety of teaching contexts.

SELECTED BIBLIOGRAPHY

Preface and Chapter 1: Where Do You Live?

Ferguson, Marilyn. *The Aquarian Conspiracy: Personal and Social Transformation in Our Time*. Los Angeles: J. P. Tarcher, Inc., 1980.

Fox, Matthew. *A Spirituality Named Compassion*. San Francisco: Harper & Row, 1979, 1990.

——. *Original Blessing*. Santa Fe, N.M.: Bear & Company, 1983.

Shea, John. *The Challenge of Jesus*. Chicago: Thomas More Press, 1975.

Teilhard de Chardin, Pierre. *The Divine Milieu*. New York: Harper & Row, 1960.

Vatican Council II. *The Conciliar and Post Conciliar Documents*. Austin Flannery, general editor. Northport, N.Y.: Costello Publishing Company, 1975.

Chapter 2: Come and See

Otto, Rudolph. *The Idea of the Holy*. New York: Oxford University Press, 1958.

Payne, Richard J., general editor. *The Classics of Western Spirituality*. New York/Ramsey/Toronto: Paulist Press, 1978–1991.

√Welch, John, O. Carm. *Spiritual Pilgrims: Carl Jung and Teresa of Avila*. New York/Ramsey: Paulist Press, 1982.

Whitson, Robley Edward. *The Center Scriptures: The Core Christian Experiences*. Bristol, Ind.: United Institute (Wyndham Hall Press), 1979, 1987.

Chapter 3: Spirituality for the Edge of an Age

Botts, Timothy R. *Sunday Doorposts: Sixty Calligraphic Renderings of Biblical Texts*. Kansas City, Mo.: Sheed and Ward, 1987.

De Mello, Anthony. *The Song of the Bird*. Garden City, N.Y.: Doubleday Image Books, 1982.

Fox, Matthew. *Meditations with Meister Eckhart: A Centering Book*. Santa Fe, N.M.: Bear & Company, 1983.

Hays, Edward. *Prayers for the Domestic Church*. Easton, Kans.: Forest of Peace Books, 1979.

————. *Pray All Ways*. Easton, Kans.: Forest of Peace Books, Inc., 1981.

————. *Prayers for a Planetary Pilgrim*. Easton, Kans.: Forest of Peace Books, 1988.

Keating, Thomas. *Open Mind, Open Heart: The Contemplative Dimension of the Gospels*. Warwick, N.Y.: Amity House, 1986.

Kozak Pat, CSJ, and Janet Schaffran, CDP *More Than Words*. A Meyer-Stone Book. New York: Crossroad, 1986.

Loder, Ted. *Guerillas of Grace: Prayers for the Battle*. San Diego, Calif.: LuraMedia, 1984.

Lonergan, Anne, and Caroline Richards, eds. *Thomas Berry and the New Cosmology*. Mystic, Conn.: Twenty-Third Publications, 1987.

Meister Eckhart. *Essential Sermons, Commentaries, Treatises and Defenses*. Trans. and intro. Edmund College, OSA, and Bernard McGinn. *The Classics of Western Spirituality*. Richard Payne, general editor. New York/Ramsey/Toronto: Paulist Press, 1978–91.

Shea, John. *Stories of God*. Chicago: Thomas More Press, 1978.

Winter, Miriam Therese. *WomanPrayer, WomanSong*. New York: Crossroad, 1986.

Video

Berry, Thomas. *Befriending the Earth: A Theology of Reconciliation between Humans and the Earth*. VHS 13-tape series. Twenty-Third Publications (185 Willow Street, Mystic, CT 06355), 1990.

Canticle to the Cosmos with Brian Swimme. VHS 12-tape series. Brian Swimme and Bruce Bochte, directors. Newstory Project, 134 Coleen Street, Livermore, CA 94550. San Francisco: Tides Foundation, 1990.

Audio

✓Sparough, J. Michael, SJ. *Body at Prayer I.* 2 tapes. Cincinnati: St. Anthony Messenger Press, Audio Cassettes (1615 Republic Street, Cincinnati, OH 45210), 1988.

✓——. *Body at Prayer II.* 2 tapes. Cincinnati: St. Anthony Messenger Press, 1989.

✓——. *The Body at Eucharist: Gesture and Posture.* 3 tapes. Cincinnati: St. Anthony Messenger Press, 1990.

✓——. *The Body at Eucharist: Senses and Symbols.* 2 tapes. Cincinnati: St. Anthony Messenger Press, 1990.

Music

Autumn, George Winston. Wyndham Hill Records (Box 9388, Stanford, CA 94305), 1982.

December, George Winston. Wyndham Hill Records (Box 9388, Stanford, CA 94305), 1982.

✓*Gentle Night: Music for Christmas and Advent*, St. Louis Jesuits. Phoenix: North American Liturgy Resources (10802 N. 23rd Avenue, Phoenix, AZ 85029), 1977.

Mystery, Rory Cooney. MYS COO. North American Liturgy Resources (10802 N. 23rd Avenue, Phoenix, AZ 85029), 1987.

Night of Silence, Marty Haugen. CS-187. GIA Publications, Inc. (7404 South Mason Avenue, Chicago, IL 60638), 1987.

✓*Shepherd Me, O God*, Marty Haugen. CS185. GIA Publications, Inc. (7404 South Mason Avenue, Chicago, IL 60638), 1987.

Sound Faith: Chants Used at the Shalem Institute, Isabella Bates (2303 Chain Bridge Road, NW, Washington, DC 20016), 1989.

Chapter 5: Come Aside and Rest Awhile/Take Two

Deshaies, Robert J. *Coming Alive in Faith: A Gospel-Based Program for Spiritual Awakening.* Coral Springs, Fla.: Jeremiah Press, 1989.

Guzie, Tad. *The Book of Sacramental Basics.* New York/Ramsey: Paulist Press, 1981.

Chapter 6: One in Mind and Heart

Brueggemann, Walter, et al. *To Act Justly, Love Tenderly, Walk Humbly: An Agenda for Ministers*. New York/Mahwah: Paulist Press, 1986.

Campbell, Peter A., Ph.D., and Edwin M. McMahon, Ph.D. *BioSpirituality: Focusing as a Way to Grow*. Chicago: Loyola University Press, 1985.

Fiand, Barbara. *Releasement: Spirituality for Ministry*. New York: Crossroad, 1987.

Grant, W. Harold, Magdala Thompson, and Thomas E. Clarke. *From Image to Likeness: A Jungian Path in the Gospel Journey*. New York/Ramsey: Paulist Press, 1983.

Houston, Jean. *The Search for the Beloved*. Los Angeles: J. P. Tarcher, Inc., 1987.

Video

Broccolo, Rev. Gerard. "New Ways of Understanding Ministry." Address delivered at the Future of the American Church Conference, Washington D.C., September 17, 1988. Available on VHS and audio cassette from Chesapeake Audiovideo Communications, Inc., 6330 Howard Lane, Elkridge, MD 21227.

Canticle to the Cosmos, part 5, "Destruction and Loss." Brian Swimme. VHS Newstory Project (134 Coleen Street, Livermore, CA 94550), 1990.

Music

As Water to the Thirsty. David Haas. GIA Publications, Inc. (7404 South Mason Avenue, Chicago IL 60638), 1987.

Come to Set Us Free. Paul Inwood. London: St. Thomas More Press, 1985. Distributed by Oregon Catholic Press, 5536 NE Hassalo, Portland, OR 97213.

Earth Spirit. (Native American Flute Music), Carlos Nakai. Canyon Records, 4143 N. 16th Street, Phoenix, AZ 85016.

Music of Taizé. "Laudate," "Alleluia," etc. Available from Credence Cassettes, National Catholic Reporter Publishing Company, Inc., 115 E. Armour Blvd., PO Box 419491, Kansas City, MO 64141-6491.

O Great Spirit. Robert Gass. Sprung Hill Music, 5216 Sunshine Canyon, Boulder, CO 80302.

Peace in the Puzzle: Solo Harp Compositions. Amy Shrove. MLC 7011. Meadowlark Records (distributed by Sparrow Corporation, Chatsworth, CA 91311), 1986.

Ritual Songs. (Native American) Salina Star, Rt. Gold Hill, Boulder, CO 80302.

Wave Tones. Jon Shore LU41. Light Unlimited Publishing (4747 E. Thomas Road, Phoenix, AZ 85018), 1988.

Chapter 7: Season of Refreshment

Brueggemann, Walter. *The Prophetic Imagination.* Philadelphia: Fortress Press, 1978.

Ferder, Fran. *Words Made Flesh: Scripture, Psychology and Human Communication.* Notre Dame, Ind.: Ave Maria Press, 1986.

Mayer, Laurence. *Evening Prayer: The Leader's Book.* Chicago: LTP, 1981.

———. *Morning Prayer: The Leader's Book.* Chicago: LTP, 1981.

———. *Morning and Evening Prayer in the Parish.* Chicago: Liturgy Training Publications, 1985.

Steindl-Rast, Brother David. *Gratefulness, the Heart of Prayer: An Approach to Life in Fullness.* New York/Ramsey: Paulist Press, 1984.

Video

The Global Brain, Peter Russell. VHS. Penny Price Productions (670 El Medio Avenue, Pacific Palisades, CA 90272), 1983.

Music

Missa Gaia. (Earth Mass), LMRC 2 Paul Winter. 2 Tapes. Living Music Records, Inc. (Box 72, Litchfield, CT 06759), 1982.

The Steadfast Love. STL-SLJ-CS St. Louis Jesuits. 2 Tapes. North American Liturgy Resources (10802 N. 23rd Avenue, Phoenix, AZ 85029), 1985.

Winter into Spring. George Winston. Wyndham Hill Records (Box 9388, Stanford, CA 94305), 1982.

WomanSong. Miriam Therese Winter, ASCAP (Medical Mission Sisters, 77 Sherman Street, Hartford, CT 06105), 1987.

Chapter 8: Greater Things Than I Shall You Do

Abesamis, Carlos H. *A Third Look at Jesus*. Quezon City, Philippines: Claretian Publications, 1988.

Baranowski, Arthur. *Creating Small Faith Communities*. Cincinnati: St. Anthony Messenger Press, 1988.

———. *Pastoring the Pastors*. Cincinnati: St. Anthony Messenger Press, 1988.

———. *Praying Alone and Praying Together*. Cincinnati: St. Anthony Messenger Press, 1988.

Bergan, Jacqueline Syrup, and S. Marie Schwan. *Take and Receive Series: A Guide for Prayer*. 5 vols. Winona, Minn.: Saint Mary's Press (Christian Brothers Publications), 1985–88.

Caprio, Betsy, and Thomas H. Hedberg. *Coming Home: A Handbook for Exploring the Sanctuary Within*. Mahwah, N.J.: Paulist Press, 1986.

———. *Coming Home: A Manual for Spiritual Direction*. Mahwah, N.J.: Paulist Press, 1986.

Deshaies Robert, Chet Stokloza, and Susan Blum. *Evangelization*. Boca Raton, Fla.: Jeremiah Press, 1988.

Durka, Gloria, et al. *Companions for the Journey: Meditation Guides on Christian Spirituality*. 6 vols. Winona, Minn.: Saint Mary's Press, 1989–91.

Groome, Thomas H. *Christian Religious Education*. New York: Harper & Row Publishers, 1980.

Huelsman, Richard J., SJ. *PRAY: Moderator's Manual*. New York/Ramsey: Paulist Press, 1976.

———. *PRAY: Participant's Handbook*. New York/Ramsey: Paulist Press, 1976.

Lynn, Matthew, Dennis Linn, and Sheila Fabricant. *Prayer Course for Healing Life's Hurts*. New York/Ramsey: Paulist Press, 1983.

Rupp, Joyce. *The Star in My Heart: Experiencing Sophia, Inner Wisdom*. San Diego, Calif.: LuraMedia, 1990.

Selner, Edward C. *Mentoring: The Ministry of Spiritual Kinship*. Notre Dame, Ind.: Ave Maria Press, 1990.

Audio

Stages of Faith, James W. Fowler, 8 sound cassettes and instruction book. St. Louis: Credence Cassettes, 1985.

In Addition:

Thought-provoking feature-length films, available on video cassettes, in the areas of lived-out spiritually include:

Babette's Feast, VHS 5046. Orion Home Video (540 Madison Avenue, New York, NY 10022), 1991.

Jesus of Montreal, OR5057. Orion Home Video (540 Madison Avenue, New York, NY 10022), 1991.

The Mission, VHS 11639. Warner Home Video (4000 Warner Blvd., Burbank, CA 91522), 1986.

✓*Romero*, VM 5228, Paulist Pictures, 1989.

An excellent mail order source for music and teaching tapes:

Credence Cassettes, 115 E. Armour Blvd., PO Box 419491, Kansas City, MO 64141-6491.

Time Consultant Conferences in Washington, D.C., particularly the "Future of the American Church Series," provide an excellent opportunity to come in touch with some current trends in theological, spiritual, and pastoral thought. To receive brochures on upcoming conferences and speakers, write:

Time Consultants, 650 Richie Highway, Severna Park, MD 21146; (301) 647-8145